AMAZING
CATS

PAUL LENZ

Thoughtplay

ISBN 978-1-9163213-2-8 (print)
ISBN 978-1-9163213-3-5 (ebook)

Published by Thoughtplay Ltd
www.thoughtplay.com

Editor: Andrew Chapman
Typeset by Prepare to Publish Ltd
www.preparetopublish.com

Cover picture: Poppycat by David Whiteland (beholder.uk)

Contents

This book is dedicated to Houdini-cat, the injured stray who came to live with me during lockdown, and to the staff of the Beaumont Veterinary Practice in Oxford for their kindness and support on his long road to recovery.

Acknowledgements

Massive thanks are due to Andrew Chapman, my friend and partner in these projects for his advice, editing and typesetting, and to Helen for her love and support. This book couldn't have been written without the various cats I have lived with (both officially and unofficially): Sooty, Carpetcat, Swiss, Wumpuss, Kittencat, Poppycat and Houdini-cat. And also the local cats who allow me to fuss them:[1] little grey cat, near wall cat (aka little black cat), grumpy wall cat, far wall cat, new wall cat, boat cat, nervous boat cat, rare boat cat, Upper Fisher cat, shouty Osney cat, ginger Osney cat, big-tail cat, floof-cat, Blanketcat, and many others...

---

[1] Yes, I have assigned names to the cats I meet in the local area. Haven't you?

A History of Domestic Cats

I f you have ever lived with cats – or even if you haven't – it probably seems like the most natural thing in the world that they should be willing and happy to share a home with humans. But if you stop and think about it for a minute, isn't it actually a little weird?

Dogs living with humans is perhaps a little easier to understand. After all, we have bred them and trained them over thousands of years to do useful things like hunt, guard and herd – and we still train them to this day, even if they aren't working dogs. Cats have been kept to keep down pests, for sure, but that isn't something we have trained them to do, they have done it because of the plentiful supply of tasty mice. Were those mice to vanish then it is likely that the cats would as well. Unless, of course, they could simply persuade the humans to feed them instead...

So how *did* it begin? The short answer is, we aren't sure. But what follows is the best guess (at the moment). First off, let's talk a little bit about the evolutionary history of cats. All living cat species today, from the tiniest house cat to the largest tiger are members of the family *Felidae,* and as such they all share a number of characteristics, including:

- They have highly sensitive whiskers
- They have excellent, large, binocular eyes
- The nose extends slightly beyond the lower jaw
- They can extend and retract their claws
- They cannot detect the sweetness of sugar, because they lack the sweet taste receptor (not many people are aware of this)

The first cats are believed to have appeared a little over 30 million years ago, with the earliest known 'true' cat found in the fossil record being *Proailurus*, who lived around 25 million years ago in Europe and Asia. The now extinct *Proailurus* was not much larger than the average domestic cat of today, weighing in at around 9 kg (20 pounds), and it is believed that they were the ancestor of all of the cat species living on the Earth today.

The domestic cat is *Felis catus,* a member of genus *Felis* along with the sand cat, the Chinese mountain cat, the black-footed cat, the African wildcat, the jungle cat and the European wildcat, all of whom genetically diverged from a common ancestor at various times over the course of the last four million years. Some of these species are still sufficiently genetically similar that they can cross-breed with each other – indeed cross-breeding with domestic cats is a significant threat to the survival of the European wildcat.

When did cats and humans start living together? Again, we are not really sure. In 2004 archeologists working on a dig site on the Mediterranean island of Cyprus found the skeletons of a cat and a human buried together in a grave that was 9,500 years old. Now, you may be thinking 'Well, that doesn't prove that cats and humans were living together, someone could have simply chucked the dead cat in when they were filling in the grave'. Leaving aside the fact that that would have been a pretty odd thing to do (or perhaps not odd for someone who lived 9,500 years ago, who knows?), the cat hadn't simply been thrown into a hole. Its body had been laid out in its own tiny grave, a mere 40cm away from the human, and it had been aligned in the same westward direction as the human body. This was a considered, deliberate act. The fact that the cat was only around eight months old also raises the (depressing for cat-lovers) possibility that the cat had been killed when its human had died so that the two could be laid to rest together.

Then there is the fact that cats are not native to Cyprus – they would have to have been brought there by humans on boats. Could some cats have snuck aboard a boat, unnoticed? That seems pretty unlikely – 9,500 years ago boats were dugout canoes or small vessels of woven reeds so there wouldn't have been much space for a cat to conceal itself for the duration of the voyage. This ancient grave cat was not a domestic cat as we would know it; rather, it was a tamed African wildcat. Nonetheless it can definitely lay claim to be the oldest known house cat.

We can be pretty sure then that cats and humans have been living together for the best part of 10,000 years – possibly much longer. Dogs, on the other hand, have definitely been living with humans for more than 14,000 years, and possibly as long as 36,000 years. (In case you were wondering, goats, pigs, sheep, and cattle are believed to have been domesticated 10-11,000 years ago; horses 5,500 years ago).[1] As I mentioned earlier, there is still something weird about the domestication of cats. Most of the other animals we have domesticated already lived in either packs or herds. Pack animals have dominance hierarchies with obvious leaders. Put simply, if a human can supplant the alpha dog then the other dogs will follow them. Pack animals were already used to living in large groups, their migrations mostly driven by the hunt for fresh grazing. If you provide them with sufficient food then you can corral and control them fairly easily.

Cats are very different beasts. They are primarily solitary hunters who come together to mate. As anyone with an outdoor cat knows, they are *very* territorial and will challenge any other puss who wanders onto their home turf. It is highly unlikely that ancient humans caught and trained cats to be useful companions. What seems most likely, as I suggested at the beginning, is that as humans developed agriculture and established settlements, and (most importantly) grain stores, so they also created the ideal conditions for mice and other rodents to live and thrive.

The first 'domestic' cats would have hung around the edges of those early villages and towns, preying on mice, rats and other vermin. Initially they would have been wary of humans. We know that today's European wildcats, even if raised by humans from kittens, are both nervous of, and aggressive towards, people. Then evolution would have kicked into play. If a random genetic mutation arose that made a cat less fearful of humans then the

---

[1] Yeah, horses come in pretty late. Weird considering how useful they are for riding on and pulling things and such like. I really should look into that more, but that is probably a topic for another book. Actually it is *definitely* a topic for another book.

beasts that possessed it would likely have a better chance of survival than those who didn't. Why? Well they would have hung around the grain stores for longer, continuing to hunt, while others had fled at the approach of the villagers. They would have started venturing into houses to hunt down the rodents that lived there, and also been able to feast upon discarded scraps. They would have been better able to find warmth and shelter during storms and winter months.

There is good evidence to suggest that domestic cats have evolved to like (well, perhaps not always 'like' let's say 'tolerate') human company. If you cross-breed a European wildcat (who, as mentioned above, really don't like humans) with a domestic cat[2] then the resulting offspring will be much more relaxed around people.

Our ancestors would have readily seen the benefit in having these furry creatures wandering around, though perhaps they saw more in cats than simply their utility. Put simply, cats just look cute to us, and probably always have. To be more specific, cats have flat faces with little snubby noses, large eyes, a high forehead, all very similar to something we have evolved to find super-cute: a human baby.

It is also possible that something else is going on as well. Something that sounds both unpleasant and outlandish: cats and humans are both being psychologically manipulated by a parasite. A parasite, as you probably know, is an organism that is adapted to live on or in another organism (the host), causing it harm in the process. Fleas, for example, are parasites that are shared by both cats and humans, but they aren't the ones that might be messing with our minds.

Toxoplasma gondii is (deep breath) an obligate intracellular parasitic one-celled eukaryote.[3] What does that mean? Well, as the name suggests, it is a tiny, single-celled organism that lives inside its hosts. It can live in pretty much any warm-blooded animal, but it can only reproduce sexually in cats (it can reproduce asexually in

---

[2] Please, don't try this cross-breeding at home.

[3] The author of this book has an honest-to-god degree in biology and he still had to look up what this meant. To be fair, he did do his degree a *long* time ago.

other hosts). The parasite gets transmitted through a cat eating the infected tissue of another animal. The parasitic cysts in the tissue burst open in the gut of the cat, realising bradyzoites (yes, that is their real name!) which infect the cells of the cat's gut wall. There they reproduce, creating oocysts which are excreted with the cat's faeces. Back out in the world they infect other animals who accidentally consume them. No, to be crude about it, you don't need to eat cat shit to get infected, these cysts are hardened survivors which can last for more than a year in the open. Just a single one needs to be on a poorly washed piece of fruit, or transferred to the mouth by someone touching their face, to cause an infection.

Okay, so that is all well and good (actually, it is pretty unpleasant) but what the heck does that have to do with mind control? Well, experiments have shown that rats and mice that are infected with *Toxoplasma gondii* become more reckless – specifically they stop avoiding the smell of cat urine. Uninfected rodents, quite under-standably, avoid areas that smell of cat urine (because where there is cat urine, there tends to be cats, and for rodents cats are a whole heap of no-fun[4]). Infected ones don't mind it. In fact one experiment found that rats would actively choose an area that smelt of cat urine over one that smelt of rabbit urine. That is clearly not great for the rats, but it is pretty awesome for the parasite – the rats are much more likely to get eaten by the cat, and hence the parasite is much more likely to infect a new cat-host.

Fair enough, you may be thinking, rats and mice are, let's be honest, pretty simple creatures.[5] Humans are highly intelligent, sentient creatures.[6] We have invented fast-breeder nuclear reactors,[7] Tik-Tok, quantum computing and microwaveable Pop-

---

[4] I thought that this was more subtle than saying 'terrifying avatars of slaughter'.

[5] Actually they are pretty smart. Rats, in particular are noted for their intelligence and are probably smarter than dogs. They also have been proven to display empathy. Given the choice between eating a tasty snack and helping a distressed rat who was treading water the majority of rats would ignore the food and go and help the other rat. We think that they deserve a better reputation.

[6] (Terms and conditions apply.)

[7] This is an incredibly subtle reference to the film *Time Bandits*. Did you get it? Really? Well done. It also means that you are scarily similar to me. I would suggest that you seek help but decades of experience suggests that none is available to you.

Tarts®: there is no way this singled-celled thingummyjig is going to change the way we behave!

Wrong.

There have been numerous, large-scale studies comparing populations of people infected with *Toxoplasma gondii* to those who are parasite free. And the findings are pretty astonishing. Very much like rats and mice, those who are infected tend to show more reckless behaviour – they are 2.65 times more likely to be involved in a car accident, for example. Infected men are more likely to ignore rules, be jealous, be suspicious, and also (perhaps relatedly) be significantly more likely to become entrepreneurs and set up their own businesses. Infected women, in contrast, tend to be more outgoing, warm hearted, and conscientious than their uninfected peers. Some people believe (though, I must stress, this has not been scientifically proven) that infected people *tend to like cats more* than uninfected people. Now, cats are unlikely to end up eating a person, so getting us to live together is unlikely to spread the parasite in that manner. However cats and people living together means that there are likely to be a lot more cats overall, which would be good for the parasite.

To be clear, *Toxoplasma gondii* has no intelligence; it didn't think, 'Hey, if I get cats and people to live together then things are gonna turn out great for me!'[8] No. But if, through random mutation, one of these little critters acquired the ability to make humans and cats live together then there is a good chance that it would do better than its fellow parasites, and as a result its genes would slowly spread and dominate the population.

In case you are now wondering if *your* behaviour has been affected by this parasite, then the answer is somewhere between 'maybe' and 'probably'.[9] Globally somewhere between 50 and 80% of people are infected with *Toxoplasma gondii* and in specific countries it can be even higher (in France, for example, infection rates have been estimated as being as high as 84%).[10]

---

[8] Natural selection is clever like that. By which I mean it isn't clever at all. It is just the continuous, brutal application of chance and time and scarce resources.

[9] If you are reading this book then I am prepared to bet cash money that you are more of a 'probably' than a 'maybe'.

[10] The author feels that he is obligated to point out that, having lived with cats for

Cats in Ancient Egypt

The ancient Egyptians are famous for their worship and veneration of cats. The earliest evidence of this relationship dates from the First Dynasty of Egypt almost 5,000 years ago when the cat-headed goddess Mafdet was worshipped. Mafdet was known for protecting the pharaohs against poisonous animals such as snakes and scorpions, a role that real-life cats would most likely have performed. She was also reputed to tear the hearts out of criminals and drop them at the feet of the pharaoh, much as a cat will present a dead mouse to their human today.

Mafdet was not the only cat-related god in the Eygptian pantheon. She was followed by Bastet (better known in the West as Bast). Originally Bast was a fierce, lion-headed warrior goddess but over the course of a couple of thousand years (yes, a couple of *thousand* years – ancient Eygptian civilisation lasted a very long time indeed)[11] she mellowed somewhat and became represented more in the form of a domestic cat – or as a woman with the head of a domestic cat. In this new form she was a goddess of fertility and pregnancy probably because cats were seen to be good mothers to their kittens, taking great care over feeding and protecting them. It is also likely that because cats have *lots* of kittens they were seen to be particularly good animals to worship if you wanted to have lots of children. For similar reasons the mother goddess Mut was also sometimes depicted as a cat (or being with a cat).

Why were the Egyptians so crazy about cats? Well, for starters, as we have already learned, they lived in a place that had lots of small, verminous animals and cats were very good and hunting down and killing these. Of course, the cats would have been doing this out of sense of self-preservation, but it is easy to imagine that the Egyptians could have also seen this as the cats protecting

decades, he is almost certainly infected with *Toxoplasma gondii*. Has this affected his behaviour, causing him to, well, love cats more than he would otherwise? No idea. Do I care if this does turn out to be the reason I love cats so much? No. Not at all.
[11] It is easy to forget how relatively fleeting our existing societies are, and how persistent many of the ones that preceded us have been. No attempt at being funny here, just an existential reflection.

humans. Much more importantly though, cats kill rats and mice. Grains such as wheat and barley were a major part of Egyptian agriculture and if you grow grain, then you need somewhere to store it once it has been harvested. Every village would have had a grain silo of some kind, as did temples and palaces. Some stores that have been excavated in recent years are vast and would have held tonnes of grain.

Although the regular annual flooding of the Nile river was well understood and forecast by the Egyptians, there would occasionally be poor years when crop yields were much lower, so maintaining large stores of grain was essential to prevent famine. There is even a story in the Old Testament whereby Joseph made a tidy profit by building up such supplies and selling them during a famine:[12]

> ... he gathered up all the food of the seven years when there was plenty in the land of Egypt, and stored up food in the cities... And Joseph stored up grain in great abundance, like the sand of the sea, until he ceased to measure it, for it could not be measured. So when the famine had spread over all the land, Joseph opened all the storehouses and sold to the Egyptians.

Where you have large amounts of grain sitting around for years it is pretty likely that you are going to get large numbers of rats and mice. After all, the closest human equivalent to being a mouse in one of those grain silos is being at an all-you-can-eat buffet that lasts for eternity. As with the earlier domestication, the first Egyptian cats probably started hanging around because it was an easy way to get a meal. It wasn't long before their value was noticed and the locals began to actively breed[13] and house them.

Much like humans today, Egyptians cared deeply about their cats. When Prince Thutmose died almost 3,400 years ago he was buried with his pet cat, who had been mummified and placed its own beautiful sarcophagus:

---

[12] Yes, this was probably the start of the futures market.

[13] I say they 'bred' the cats; it wasn't really very sophisticated. They just got un-neutered toms and queens (we'll explain this term later) together and let nature take its course.

Thutmose may well have achieved great things in life, but today he is best known for the grave of his cat. Even older cat tombs[14] have been found, some with small pots that are believed to have originally contained milk for the cats to lap at in the afterlife.

This level of veneration didn't always turn out great for the cats themselves though. It's true that cats were subject to great protection by law – killing or injuring one was a serious crime. Indeed the Greek historian Diodorus Siculus tells the story of a Roman citizen who was lynched by an Egyptian mob around 60 BC for (accidentally) killing a cat:

> And whoever intentionally kills one of these animals is put to death, unless it be a cat or an ibis that he kills; but if he kills one of these, whether intentionally or unintentionally, he is certainly put to death, for the common people gather in crowds and deal with the perpetrator most cruelly, sometimes doing this without waiting for a trial... So deeply implanted also in the hearts of the common people is their

---

[14] Catacombs, anyone?

superstitious regard for these animals and so unalterable are the emotions cherished by every man regarding the honour... when one of the Romans killed a cat and the multitude rushed in a crowd to his house, neither the officials sent by the king to beg the man off nor the fear of Rome which all the people felt were enough to save the man from punishment, even though his act had been an accident.'[15]

Despite these laws it seems as though there must have been some loopholes when it came to the killing of cats. Mummified cats were often given by pilgrims as offering to their gods. And when I say often, I really mean *often*. In just the single cemetery of Beni Hasan in central Egypt more than *200,000* mummified cats were found. Most of these were then shipped to Liverpool ground up, and used as fertilizer. We can't be certain, but we are pretty sure that the Egyptians who went to all of that trouble mummifying those cats thousands of years ago would have been pretty upset to learn that they ended up being ploughed into damp English fields. Whatever their ultimate fate, there is no way that these were all cats who died peacefully in old age of natural causes. They would have been bred, and then killed, to supply the pilgrim industry. Given their beliefs about human mummification it is quite possible that the people involved thought that this was okay,[16] as the cats would be heading to some glorious cat afterlife. While I would like to give them the benefit of the doubt, frankly the idea of anyone killing a cat, whatever their belief system, is something I find pretty upsetting.

That isn't to say that cats were not much loved in ancient Egypt. The Greek historian Herodotus wrote that when a cat died all of the (human) inhabitants of the house would shave off their eyebrows to show that they were in mourning. Once their eyebrows had grown back this period of grief was considered to be formally over. This may seem a little extreme, but wait till you hear what he reports they do when the household *dog* dies:

---

[15] This is very hard, yes, but how do you *accidentally* kill a cat? After all, there weren't any cars, he didn't run it over. Sure, there were carts and such like but as some kind of noble Roman citizen he would probably have been riding in one, not driving it.

[16] For the record, I absolutely do *not* think that breeding cats so that you can then kill them and wrap them in bandages is okay. But yes, those were different times...

And in whatever houses a cat has died by a natural death, all those who dwell in this house shave their eyebrows only, but those in whose houses a dog has died shave their whole body and also their head.

I have to confess that I was a little bit, well, disappointed when I read this. After all, I had thought that Egyptians loved cats *the best* but if one uses the measure of 'amount of hair shaved off upon death' it is pretty clear that the dogs are ahead. A shaven head at that.[17]

Perhaps the most extraordinary Egyptian cat story relates to the Battle of Pelusium in 525 BC when King Cambyses the Second of Persia invaded Egypt seeking that country's throne.[18] As the two armies faced each other, with battle about to commence, Cambyses ordered his troops to... bring forward armfuls of live cats (while they were Persian cats they probably weren't *Persian cats* as we would know them today) and put them on the ground in front of them. The Egyptians, so fearful of injuring the cats, refused to fire their arrows at the enemy and were brutally defeated. Full disclosure, it wasn't *just* cats that the Persians used, but I like to think that they were the most important animals:

When Cambyses attacked Pelusium, which guarded the entrance into Egypt, the Egyptians defended it with great resolution. They advanced formidable engines against the besiegers, and hurled missiles, stones, and fire at them from their catapults. To counter this destructive barrage, Cambyses ranged before his front line dogs, sheep, cats, ibises, and whatever other animals the Egyptians hold sacred.[19] The Egyptians immediately stopped their operations, out of fear of hurting the animals, which they hold in great veneration. Cambyses captured Pelusium, and thereby opened up for himself the route into Egypt. – Polyaenus, *Stratagems*, Book 7

---

[17] Sorry.

[18] Spoiler, he like *totally* ended up getting it.

[19] It is a good story, but I have to wonder why the cats hung around after being released. They were in the middle of a *freaking battlefield*! In my experience cats tend to hang around around because there is a good chance of them getting one (or more) of the following: some food, some milk, a fuss, a nice warm place to sleep, something to play with. It doesn't seem hugely likely that any of those things were going to present themselves in the middle of an Egyptian battlefield.

No mention is made of what happened to this feline shield after the battle – if they were anything like the cats I have known they would have got the hell out of there as soon as trouble kicked off.[20]

It is worth nothing that the source for this story is the Macedonian retired general and author Polyaenus, who was writing almost 700 years after the battle took place. The great historian Herodotus who wrote about the battle less than a century after it took place makes no mention of the use of cats. Maybe he just wasn't a cat person?[21]

Cats in Greece and Rome

The Roman and Greek empires coexisted with that of Egypt for many centuries, so you might have expected them to have adopted similar attitudes towards cats. Okay, perhaps not the whole 'worshipping them as gods and executing people who kill them' part of it, but certainly the 'having them around to kill rats and mice' thing. In reality house cats were very rare in ancient Greece and Rome. It has been suggested that there was an Egyptian law that forbade the export of cats and that soldiers were even sent out to retrieve kitties that had been smuggled to other countries. Despite this being asserted as a fact in a number of places online I have been unable to track down a reliable source for it. It *may* be true, but we can't be certain.

A Roman mosaic of a cat catching a partridge

[20] Or, was it, as the earlier footnote suggests, *before* everything kicked off, the second they got free.
[21] Yeah, but we did learn about the whole dead-cat-eyebrow-mourning thing from him a little earlier.

A good reason for suspecting that there was no prohibition on the export of cats is that we know for a fact there were domestic cats in ancient Greece at least as early as the mid-fifth century BC. Two coins from that era have been found showing Iokastos and Phalanthos, the founders of Rhegion and Taras, playing happily with their pet cats. These two seemed to be unusual in their feline affections. Rats and mice were a problem for the Greeks and the Romans, much as they were for the Egyptians, but they addressed it by keeping pet weasels[22] and ferrets. In the remains of the city of Pompeii, which was destroyed in AD79, hardly any cat bones have been found.[23] Those that do appear to be from strays, there weren't yet being kept as pets. As the centuries passed however it became clearer to the Romans that cats were simply better (and, I would argue) nicer to have around to solve rodent problems and they replaced weasels in the household.[24]

Rats weren't just a problem in Roman homes, they were also a problem for the Roman army – eating food stores and chewing through equipment. Military settlements across the empire acquired their own cats, who were treated with respect and affection by the soldiers.

Cats in East Asia

Evidence has been found of cats living around humans in China around 5,300 years ago. It is not clear that they were what we would consider to be domesticated cats, but the handful of bones recovered from an ancient refuse pit indicate that they were smaller than wild cats and much more likely to be similar to the domesticated cats that were living in Egypt at the same time. It is possible that the practice of keeping cats spread from Africa to Asia, or that it emerged independently in both places – we simply can't be sure. Certainly by around 2,000 years ago cats were widely kept in ancient China and held in considerable regard. This has caused some people to wonder

---

[22] How do you tell the difference between a weasel and a stoat? The stoat actually *is* a weasel – the short-tailed weasel. No joke here!

[23] It is possible, however, that the cats knew what was coming and got the hell out of there. See the later story about a Japanese tsunami...

[24] We're not currently planning an *Amazing Weasels* book in this series.

why the cat is not one of the 12 animals of the Chinese zodiac. There is a myth that says the animals were chosen by the Jade Emperor by holding a race – the first 12 to finish would be selected. As the cat was nocturnal and would normally be sleeping during the day when the race was going to be held it asked its friend the rat to wake it before the race was due to start. The rat, alas, broke its promise, leaving the cat happily snoozing, and in so doing gained a place in the zodiac itself. When the cat finally awoke it was, to put it bluntly, very cross with the rat, and swore vengeance upon it and all of its enemies. And that is why, to this day, cats are ferocious hunters of rats.[25]

A Chinese cat market in 1846

Cats spread to Japan via China, possibly as early as the sixth century, and were likely first presented as gifts to members of Japanese nobility. The kanji character for the Japanese word for cat *neko* looks like the Chinese word *kone*: 'likes rats'. They were certainly well established in the Imperial Court more than a thousand years ago. We can be sure of this because of the diary of Emperor Uda who ruled Japan from 887 through 897. The entry that he wrote on 11 March 889 is titled *For the Love of a Cat* and I think that it is really rather lovely:

---

[25] I think that really the rat brought all of this on himself. Did the cat overreact? Perhaps. But seriously, rat-dude, you made a promise to your friend!

On the 6th Day of the 2nd Month of the First Year of the Kampo era. Taking a moment of my free time, I wish to express my joy of the cat. It arrived by boat as a gift to the late Emperor, received from the hands of Minamoto no Kuwashi.

The color of the fur is peerless. None could find the words to describe it, although one said it was reminiscent of the deepest ink. It has an air about it, similar to Kanno. Its length is 5 sun, and its height is 6 sun. I affixed a bow about its neck, but it did not remain for long.

In rebellion, it narrows its eyes and extends its needles.[26] It shows its back.

When it lies down, it curls in a circle like a coin. You cannot see its feet. It's as if it were circular Bi disk.[27] When it stands, its cry expresses profound loneliness, like a black dragon floating above the clouds.[28]

By nature, it likes to stalk birds. It lowers its head and works its tail. It can extend its spine to raise its height by at least 2 sun. Its color allows it to disappear at night. I am convinced it is superior to all other cats.[29]

Uda was not the only Japanese emperor to be fond of felines. Emperor Ichijo who reigned a century later owned a beast that he named Myoby no Otodo, which translates as Chief-Lady-in Waiting-of-the Inner Palace – a very fancy title indeed! Myoby no Otodo had more than just a title – she had actual human ladies-in-waiting to tend to her needs,[30] and the emperor instructed his tailor to make tiny suits of clothing for her and her kittens. That is very sweet (we should note that this happened in the year 999 when the emperor was only 13 years old) but if Myoby was like the cats I have known I think she was probably a bit pissed off at being made to play dress-up.

No, you may be thinking 'hang on, surely *commoners* (that is

---

[26] I assume that this is synonym for 'claws'.

[27] No, I have no idea either. Could I Google it? Yes. Did I? No.

[28] Black dragons, it seems, were noted for their cries. Particularly when they were floating above clouds. The use of the word 'floating' is a bit odd, isn't it? Were they lighter than air, like a helium balloon?

[29] It turns out that many (perhaps most) people believe that the cats they live with are 'superior to all other cats'.

[30] Being waited on by humans is a tradition maintained by domestic cats to this day. They just aren't usually lucky enough to get a dozen humans to wait on each of them.

'working folks') couldn't be allowed to live in the Imperial Court of Japan?' Okay, so you *probably* weren't, but if you had been you would have been quite correct. In order for his beloved cats to live in the court Emperor Ichijo decreed that cats were not allowed to work, and they were officially part of the aristocracy, specifically the 'Fifth Order of the Court'. This life of feline leisure astonishingly lasted more than six hundred years until 1602. At that time rats and mice were causing a serious threat to Japan's crucial silk trade (they like to eat the silkworms) and so the government was forced to act. A decree was issued that made it illegal to house or feed cats, or to sell them or give them as gifts. Pretty much overnight cats were cast out of their comfortable homes and forced to fend for themselves, which must have been a bit of a shock to the kitties concerned. It would certainly have been very tough for them, but as far as the government was concerned the law worked. Without humans to feed them the cats decimated the rodent population and saved the silk trade.

These imperial cats were very distinctive in that they had very short bobtails, and they exist to this day as the Japanese bobtail breed. This distinctive feature is the result of a genetic mutation in the cats originally brought over from China. At least that is what so-called *scientists* will tell you based upon their DNA analysis and such like. The *real* reason[31] is somewhat different. Originally Japanese cats had long tails, just like all of the others. Then disaster struck. Many years ago a cat was curled up by a fire on a cold winter's day. A bit too close to the fire it turned out... Its tail caught alight and the poor kitty ran in panic through the city, accidentally setting fire to many buildings in the process. The emperor, seeing his magnificent capital reduced to ashes, was *furious*. He decreed that all cats should have their tails chopped off to ensure that it never happened again.[32]

---

[31] To be clear, this is *not* the real reason, I just like the story and wanted an excuse to tell it. At the end of the day I am with the scientists and their test-tubes on this one. Okay, not test-tubes. For DNA analysis they would most likely have been using electrophoresis gel. See! Someone *did* remember something from their biology degree!

[32] I kinda get where he was coming from, but I think that if a single cat with a flaming tail can burn down a city then you then it is probably more the fault of your urban planning than the terrified kitty. *Maybe* it would have been better to think about improving the building regulations and perhaps forming a fire brigade instead?

Another legendary Japanese cat is more fondly remembered. You may well have seen a small model cat in a shop or restaurant window (or indeed a home) with its paw raised. There are also battery and solar powered versions[33] where the paw bobs up and down waving. It actually isn't waving at you – the Japanese gesture to beckon is made by holding up the hand, palm down, and folding the fingers back and forth. That is why this is the *Maneki-neko*, the 'beckoning cat'. *Maneki-neko*[34] are believed to bring their owners good luck and there are a number of stories about why this may be the case. One is that its gesture is similar to the movement a cat makes when it is washing its face, and there is an ancient Japanese belief that when a cat washes its face a visitor is soon to arrive (I should note that if a visitor arrived every time the cats I have lived with washed their faces there wouldn't be any room left in my home). This belief possibility originated from an old Chinese proverb that says that when a cat washes its face then rain is coming. Why is rain going to bring visitors (and, indeed, be lucky)? Well, if you run a shop or inn, rain is good for business as people will come inside to shelter from it. Statues of cats washing their ears that are more than 1,500 years old have been found in China, and these could be the earliest forms of *Maneki-neko*.

There are a couple of alternative stories that may explain why this beckoning cat is considered to be lucky. One is that the 17th century samurai Li Naotaka was caught in a torrential storm and took shelter under a tree. Looking out through the rain he saw a cat sitting in a nearby temple, waving its paw in a beckoning manner. Intrigued, he headed over to the temple to find out why the cat was calling him over (or maybe because he just wanted to give the kitty a quick fuss, the story is unclear on this point). When he got to the cat the tree he had previously been sheltering under got struck by lightning; were it not for the cat, he would have surely died! Another tale tells of a poor shopkeeper who took pity upon a stray, starving cat and shared his meagre supplies of food with it.

---

33 Declaration of interest: the author owns just such a device.

34 One of the cashiers in the nearest convenience store to the author has a *Maneki-neko* tattoo on his arm. I kinda want to mention it/ask him about it, but I am too self conscious and have no idea where the conversation would go. I probably should though, right? He would probably like someone knowing what it is?

To thank him the cat would sit in his window and beckon in customers and the business flourished as a result. Whatever the truth of the story it is fair to say that if I passed a shop with a cat in the window I would probably pop in to say hello irrespective of whether or not it was actively beckoning to me.[35]

The reverence with which cats were held in Japan is maintained to this day, most notably on the island of Tashirojima. In the 18th century the silk trade here was, like many other places in Japan, a hugely important industry, and as we have learned, cats were vital to saving this trade from the attacks of rats and mice. Being an island there was no way for cats to naturally migrate to the area, so they were imported by the industrious locals and allowed to flourish. In addition to silk production fishing was an important industry on Tashirojima and this worked out well for the cats. Not only were there lots of scraps of fish lying around, the fishermen believed that the cats brought them good luck, and that the behaviour of the cats could be used to predict the weather and the locations of fish. In order to help bring in a good catch, the fishermen would ensure that the cats were well fed.

Tragedy struck one day when a cat was killed by a falling rock while the fishermen were working. The men were so upset that they buried the cat and raised a shrine to it – a *Nekoj-inja*. Over the years more shrines were built to cats and as a result there are now more than ten on this tiny island. As the fishing and silk industries slowed, so the population of the island reduced and it is now home to around 70, generally older, humans. The story is somewhat different for the cats; they are now believed to number more than 500, so many in fact that Tashirojima is now known as 'Cat Island'. Most of these cats are what we would term feral, but that does not mean that they are unloved and poorly cared for. The islanders continue to feed them and tend to their needs, with a special team of volunteers called *Nyanko Kyouwakoku*.[36] That whole notion of cats bringing good luck and wealth? Well, for the people of Tashirojima it looks like it is true. Thousands of tourists visit the

---

[35] In fact, extensive real-world research confirms that I would *definitely* go into a shop that contained a cat. Indeed, this has already happened many, many, times.
[36] If I lived there I would volunteer. In a heartbeat.

island each year to see their amazing cats![37] And what about cats predicting what is going to happen in the seas – surely that can't be true too? Well, probably not in the way that the sailors thought hundreds of years ago, but something happened fairly recently that suggests that cats can sense things in nature that are invisible to us. In 2011 the island was struck by the tsunami caused by the Tohoku earthquake (don't worry, both cats and humans got through it okay). Before the waters arrived a number of the cats were seen to be behaving very strangely,[38] yowling at things that weren't there and generally being very stressed out. Were they trying to warn the humans who had looked after them for so long? I like to think that perhaps they were.

Cats in Australasia

There isn't really very much to say about the history of cats in Australasia, basically because they don't really have much of a history. The most commonly accepted belief is that they arrived in Australia in the late 18th century with European immigrants – the earliest recorded date for their introduction is 1804, but it is quite possible that they had been around for a few decades before then. Some people maintain that they arrived on the continent as early as 1650, brought over by Malay fishermen.[39] What is certain is that the ecosystem of this previously cat-free land was not well equipped to handle the furry beasts. They spread rapidly and decimated populations of ground-nesting birds and small mammals. The only species to prey upon cats themselves in Australia are dingos and wedge-tailed eagles.[40] This means that in dingo and eagle-free areas they are the apex predator, the only limit to their population being the supply of food. As a result, while there are around 2.7 million domestic cats in Australia there are thought to be as many as *six million* feral cats.

Cats arrived in New Zealand a little earlier, arriving on Captain

---

[37] Yes, I really, really, want to go there too.

[38] There are videos online of this. The cats are behaving *very* strangely and certainly don't appear to be happy *at all*.

[39] Fishing for, specifically, sea cucumbers.

[40] They have very distinctive, wedge-shaped tails. Really. Look them up if you don't believe me.

James Cook's ship *HMS Endeavour* in 1769. The Kiwi ecology was even less prepared for them than their Aussie neighbour. Until the Māori and European peoples arrived there were no native land mammals in New Zealand (apart from three species of bat). This meant that birds didn't have any predators (apart from other birds).[41] As a result cats (and also rats) have torn through the islands leaving a trail of death behind them. So much so that there are dedicated 'cat eradication' programmes on a number of the smaller islands to protect the few remaining members of a number of rare bird species.[42]

Cats in the Middle East and West Asia

Cats are highly revered in Islam, and the prophet Muhammad was known to love the creatures. His favourite cat was named Muezza and there are numerous stories about her. One tells how she bowed to the prophet one day as he returned from the mosque; he stroked her three times in return and gave her the power to always land on her feet if she fell (we'll explore how cats land in more detail later). In another she was sleeping on the sleeve of his robe when the call to prayer sounded. Rather than move and wake the cat, Muhammad instead cut the sleeve off his robe, allowing her to continue to sleep peacefully. One of Muhammad's companions was known as *Abu Hurairah*, which literally translates as 'Father of a Kitten', a name bestowed due to his huge affection for felines. Abu Hurairah once said that Muhammad declared a woman who starved a kitten and didn't even give it water was destined to go to hell. Another companion of the prophet, Abu Saeed, reportedly owned a cat who once saved Muhammad from a poisonous snake. There is also said to be a connection between the markings on cats and Islam. Muhammad petted the cat that had saved his life from the snake and left four dark lines on its forehead. Similarly the 'M'-shaped marking on the heads of tabby cats is said to arise from him gently resting his hand on Muezza.

---

[41] Actually, the *tuatara* does eat chicks and eggs. It is a weird reptile that is the last surviving member of its order, and is sometimes called a 'living fossil'. Do check it out if you have some time.

[42] One of them is the *kakapo* – a large, flightless, adorable, parrot. If you would like to learn more about it then I suggest you read the excellent *Last Chance to See* by Douglas Adams.

Because cats are so obsessed with washing themselves they are consider in Islamic tradition to be *ritually clean*, which means that they are free to enter people's homes and even mosques. Indeed cats are so clean that water they have drunk from is permitted to be used for *wudu*, the ritual washing of the body. It isn't just Japan that has places dedicated to cats. In Aleppo, Syria, there used to be a compound known as *Jami al-Qitat*, which translates as 'Mosque of the Cats'. It is said to have been built as a cat hospital by a wealthy merchant, Osman Pasha, in 1730 to thank the feisty felines for ridding his granaries of rats and mice. Now, you might be thinking that might have been a couple of rooms and a handful of cats. If so, you are way off in terms of scale. Victorian travellers reported hundreds, sometimes even *thousands* of cats being fed each day on a special feeding ground. There was also a special nursery for kittens and a hospice for elderly cats to live out their final days in comfort. Osman Pasha left sufficient funds in his will to ensure that the operations could continue for decades after his death. This may sound like a lovely thing to you, but European visitors in the 19th century found it, well, pretty appalling. One traveller expressed surprise at the fact that the Muslims of Aleppo refused to drown kittens (as that was common practice in Europe at the time)[43] and commented:

> How strange it is, that Christianity should be harder towards animals than the inferior[44] religions, just as slavery is worst among Christian nations.

In ancient Persia the attitude to cats was somewhat different. In Zoroastrian mythology they were said to have been the unholy product of sex between the human woman Jamak and a devil. Far from being the epitome of cleanliness they were classed as a hated 'wolf species'. It was said that if a cat ate from a bowl it would still be unclean even if it had been washed seven times. Were a cat to urinate in water then it would kill all of the fishes in the sea.[45] It

---

[43] I am going to be talking about European attitudes to cats shortly. Spoiler: not great. Not great *at all*.

[44] The use of the word 'inferior' here is, of course, totally subjective.

[45] One would have hoped that the fact that there still were fish in the sea would have proved that theory wrong, unless for thousands of years cats had been *very careful indeed* about where they pissed. To be fair, other versions of this suggest that only

wasn't just fish that they could kill – if a person ate food that had been touched – even fleetingly – by the whiskers of a cat they would then waste away and die.

Despite all of these stories it seems that cats were much loved by the Persians and, as in many other places, played a valuable role in keeping down the populations of rats and mice. According to legend, this fact was once used for political advantage. King Khosrow II, who ruled Iran from in the late sixth and early seventh centuries, sent an evil man named Ray to be the governor of the city of his rival Bahram Chobin. Once settled, Ray ordered all of the cats in the city to be killed, which led to a massive explosion in the population of rats and mice. So much so that the people were forced to flee the city. The tale goes on to say that the city was ultimately saved by the queen, who gave a playful kitten to Khosrow and in so doing persuaded him to let the cats return.

Much like their contemporaries in Japan, Persian royalty at the end of the first millennium were very attached to their feline friends. Prince Rukn al-Dawla was noted for his adoration of his cat friend. So much so that when people wanted to petition him for favours they would tie their requests around the neck of his cat because in that way he was sure to see them. I are not sure about the prince's thoughts on the matter, but if someone was to tie something around the neck of a cat that *I* lived with then it would have the opposite effect of making me feel kindly towards them. One Sufi sheik was said to love his cat so much that he had tiny shoes made for it so that it could sleep on his prayer carpet without its claws damaging the costly material.[46]

Persian cats, those glorious balls of floof, have their own creation myth. The great hero Rostam[47] is said to have once saved a magician from a gang of thieves. The magician wanted to repay the man who

---

10,000 fish would die from each aquatic toilet incident.

[46] I don't think that it would have been that easy to put tiny shoes on a cat, let alone to ensure that the cat had to keep them on. I once had to put a cat in a special t-shirt after it had an operation (in order to stop it licking its stitches). That was not fun for either me or the cat. I really don't want to repeat it. Cat is doing fine now, thanks for asking.

[47] Very much like Heracles, he carried out seven labours and generally had a series of amazing adventures – check them out!

had saved his life, but Rostam told him that he had everything he desired in the world. The magician took that as a challenge, and decided to create something that the great hero had no idea that he desired. He sat by the fire and took up a handful of smoke, a pinch of fire, and reached up to grab the brightest star in the sky. He mixed them all up together and then opened his hands and there sat a perfect Persian kitten. Its soft fur like a cloud of smoke, its eyes glinting like starlight, and its tiny pink tongue like a tongue of flame. Nice man, that magician.

Cats in Europe

All around the world cats were being treated with great respect, be it having tiny bespoke outfits made for them in Japan, or miniature shoes in Persia. They surely were having a pretty good time of it in Europe too, right? Um, yes, about that... some of what follows isn't great for cats. It is thought that the Romans were responsible for spreading domestic cats across their empire with their armies, all the way up into Scotland (though it is perfectly possible that cats had already made their way to many of these places by stowing away on boats, killing mice, and generally making themselves useful. The Romans came, the Romans went, and the cats stayed. The Europeans, however, had a somewhat more troubling relationship with them than the inhabitants of, dare I say, the more civilised people in the East. To put not too fine a point on it, medieval Europeans basically *hated* cats.

Don't believe us? How about this as an example. To this day a festival takes places each year in Ypres, Belgium, called *Kattenstoet*[48] which is *devoted* to cats. There is a cat parade, people dress up (often as cats), there are simply *massive* floats that look like cats. 'Hang on,' you might think, 'you don't seem to be making a very good case here, you are talking about an adorable cat celebration!' Well, yes, today it may seem to be an adorable celebration of all things feline, but the origin of the tradition is much more gruesome. You see, *kattenstoet* ends each year with someone dressed as a jester throwing toy cats off the top of the belfry of the cloth hall[49] down to the square below.

---

[48] Literally 'Festival of the Cats'.

[49] It is pretty high up. I have seen pictures.

The reason that they throw toy cats today is because if they stuck to the original tradition they would end up getting arrested...

Originally real, live cats were thrown from the tower to their death or serious injury on the ground. It is unclear exactly how the tradition started. One theory is that over the winter the cats helped protect the wool that was stored in the hall by keeping down the mouse population. In the spring the wool was sold, the cats were no longer needed so *obviously* the *only* thing to do with them was take them up to the top of the tower and throw them off. An alternative explanation is that cats were associated with witchcraft, and by killing the cats one was also killing evil spirits. We will learn more about cats and witches in a minute, but in case you think that I am being unfair on the good people of Ypres by mentioning a gruesome tradition from the ancient past, this might shock you. The last time that real cats were thrown from the top of the tower was 1817, little more than 200 years ago.

Why did the Europeans hate cats? Well, to put it simply they thought that they were *evil*. For sure, they were handy to have around for killing mice and the like, but they really couldn't be trusted *at all*. Why was this? Well, in Christian teachings the act of a cat playing with a mouse was often likened to the way in which the devil would play with a sinner before ultimately casting them down to an eternity of damnation and torture in hell. In 1484 William Caxton wrote in his *Royal Book*:

> The devyl playeth ofte with the synnar, lyke as the catte doth with the mous.[50]

Cats were not simply considered to be allegories of the devil, some also believed that they actually were a facet of the great Satan himself, taking bestial form to represent him on earth, do dire deeds, and be worshipped by witches and heretics. The concept of cat-as-the-devil can be traced back to the 12th century and St Bartholomew of Farne. Obviously he wasn't actually a saint at that

---

[50] Bill, mate, sort out your spelling. Too many letters in 'cat', not enough in 'mouse'. Yes we *know* that you were the first person to bring a printing press to England, but that isn't an excuse.

point,[51] but that doesn't really matter. What *does* matter is that he used to fight against the devil, really quite often. In these battles the devil would take the form of a mouse. Or a lion. Or a bull. Or an ape. Or (finally) a cat. Now it may seem a little odd that only the cat got associated with the devil as a result, but the reason seems to be that the whole 'cat playing with a mouse is like the devil playing with a sinner' thing had already set people against them.

Around the same time that Bartholomew was fighting a devilish cat, the Welsh writer (and later archdeacon of Oxford) Walter Map was stoking the anti-cat fire. In his book *De nugis curialium* (which roughly translates as *Trinkets for the Court*) he wrote about the heretical activities of the Publicans[52] and the Patarines. Anyway, Map wrote of the devil-worshipping practices of these heretics. In them the devil would appear to them in the form of a black cat. After he had appeared the Satanists would then, err, extinguish all of their lamps and fumble around in the dark until they could get their hands on the cat. Having grasped the feline, sorry, the DEVIL, they would demonstrate their devotion to him by, um, *kissing him under the tail*. Whatever these people *actually* believed I have to say that you have to be pretty dedicated to kiss a cat's bum to prove it. While this probably sounds totally absurd it was very bad news for cats, and also for humans (particularly women) who liked cats. *De nugis curialium*, and manuscripts like it, played a role in defining medieval notions of witchcraft, and cats were very much a part of it.

The practice of 'black cat bum kissing'[53] astonishingly appears multiple times in the literature of the period. A few decades later Willam of Auvergne wrote in *Tractatus de fide et legibus* of Cathars and Waldensians taking turns to kiss the bottom of a black cat

---

[51] Nor was he called Bartholomew, he was called Tostig, and then he was called William. Seriously, dude, make up your mind about this whole name thing. Changing it all the time is, well, a bit *weird*.

[52] In case you were wondering, the 'Publicans' were not a group of people who ran pubs, they were followers of Arnold of Brescia (who criticised the wealth of the Catholic church). Possibly a few of them ran pubs as well. After all, innkeeper was a fairly common occupation back then, so the law of averages suggests that at least a couple of them probably were.

[53] When I started writing this book I never thought that it would include this line. Isn't research a wonderful thing?

described as being the size of a small dog (possibly he could have just said 'a cat the size of a large cat'[54]). Alan of Lille wrote of the Cathars:

> Vel Cathari dicuntur a cato, quia, ut dicitur, osculantur posteriora catti, in cujus specie, ut dicunt, apparet eis Lucifer[55]

Not long afterwards the devilish nature of cats acquired an official status that was to haunt them for centuries to come. The German preacher Konrad von Marburg claimed to have uncovered a Satanic cult that worshipped a diabolical black cat. 'Uncovered' in this context needs to have the slight caveat that the people involved confessed to their behaviour when tortured to the point of death, so maybe it wasn't *totally* true. It was, however, good enough proof for Pope Gregory IX to establish the Papal Inquisition, and to issue the decree *Vox in Rama*, which called for a crusade against such heresy.

This decree goes into some detail about the rites of the heretics. A ceremony that involved meeting a giant toad, and kissing a skinny white man, ended with a statue of a black cat coming to life. This living statue-puss would walk backwards[56] towards the participants with its tail raised in the air so that the master of the sect, and any new initiates, could *kiss it on the bum*. From then on cats in general and black ones in particular, were considered to be highly suspicious.

The specific connection between witches and cats dates from around the same time. Gervase of Tilbury, a favourite of King Henry II, wrote in his *Otia Imperialia*[57] of witches who flew through the air at night and could change their shape to take on the form

---

[54] Or even just 'a large cat'.

[55] This crudely translates as 'The Cathars kiss the bum of the devil cat'.

[56] Have you ever seen a cat walk backwards? Like, walk straight backwards? No, I didn't think so. That fact alone should have been enough to raise alarm bells about the truth behind of all these stories

[57] This literally translates as 'Recreation for an Emperor', basically an early type of encyclopedia. People may have issues with Wikipedia today, but it is orders of magnitude better than what Gervase turned out. Editing it some centuries later the philosopher Gottfriend Liebnniz described it as *a bag of foolish old woman's tales'*. Personally, I think that is putting it mildly.

of a cat. Unluckily for the cats, he also claimed that if a witch was wounded when in the shape of a cat, her injuries would remain when she re-took human form. This basically gave people free reign to abuse cats, on the off chance that some were transformed witches who they could identify later on by looking for injured women. It pretty much goes without saying that in a culture where there were high levels of spousal abuse it wasn't going to be that hard to find women with cuts and bruises and so the process appeared to confirm its own validity.

There is an extensive list of folk tales that tell some form of the 'woman and cat sharing injuries story'. From the Netherlands there is the story of a cat that has a pan of hot butter thrown over it, only to reappear as an old woman, covered in burns the following day. In both Norway and Germany tale is told of a cat that had its paw cut off, only for the following day the miller's wife to be missing a hand.[58] And other versions also exist from Wales, Austria and the USA where the woman isn't necessarily the miller's wife, but the whole severed paw/hand thing happens.

Things really came to a head in 1486 when Heinrich Kramer published the *Malleus Maleficarum*.[59] This was basically an all-purpose guide that taught you all about witches and what to do with them.[60] It was a prime text in the witch trials that, over the following centuries, resulted in around 50,000 people (mostly women, mostly over the age of 40) being burned at the stake. In the book Kramer restates the 'women as cats' myth with a story in which a man beats off an attack from three cats, only to be thrown in prison a short time later, accused of assaulting three 'matrons of the town'. Things are looking bad for this chap – he is facing a sentence of death, when the wise magistrates realise that *of course* there was some devilish connection between the women and the cats and he is quite innocent of the crimes of which he has been accused. Hurrah! As for the fate of the women, the book does not recount, but Kramer makes it perfectly clear that they were in no

---

[58] In some versions of the tale the miller's wife then gets burned alive. Along with all of her children. Nice.

[59] This is usually translated as the *Hammer of Witches*. Heinrich may have had his strengths, but it is pretty clear that subtlety wasn't one of them.

[60] Generally, torture a confession out of them. Then burn them to death.

way innocent bystanders – they had to have formed a pact with the devil. I find it hard to imagine that things worked out well for them.

You may be thinking that such absurd (and utterly horrendous) beliefs are artefacts from the distant past. If so, you may be in for a shock. The last victim of a witch hunt[61] in England was 'Dummy' the Witch of Sible Hedingham,[62] in *1863*. Yes, Victorian England with its railways, telegraphs, industry and science. And witch hunts. Poor Dummy was an elderly deaf-mute man. He worked as a fortune teller, and was accused by one Emma Smith of cursing her with a disease.[63] A drunk mob threw him in a brook, beat him with sticks, and he died as a result. Smith and a friend of hers who led the mob were caught, tried and convicted of causing his death.[64] That isn't even the last killing of a witch. In Ireland, in 1895, Bridget Clearly was beaten and burned to death by her husband because he believed that his 'real' wife had been taken away by fairies and replaced her with a witch. And in 1997 – yes *1997* – two Russian farmers killed a woman and injured five members of her family because they believed that she had used folk magic against them.

There is another reason why the English, in particular, may have hated cats – that is because a cat once attempted to overthrow the monarchy in 1318.[65] Edward II of England was not a popular king. He has been pretty useless at battling Robert the Bruce of Scotland and he just didn't seem to be very, well, *kingly.* His hobbies included digging ditches and farming, the kind of things only peasants should have been doing. One day a young clerk called John Deydras (also known as John of Powderham) knocked on the door of Beaumont Palace, the royal palace in Oxford, and claimed that actually *he* was the king, not that Edward fellow they had been following. This may seem somewhat absurd, but he did look a *lot*

---

[61] A literal witch hunt, where people actually *hunt a witch* in real life. Not a gang of people going after someone on social media.

[62] Yes, I thought that this name sounded made up too. But no, it is a real place in Essex, current population around 4,000. The parish church looks *charming.*

[63] It turned out that she had Lyme disease, which is caught from ticks, not curses. Idiots.

[64] They got six months' hard labour. Doesn't really seem just, does it?

[65] Allegedly.

like the king, except for one key feature – he was missing an ear. This wasn't a problem for John's story though; indeed, it was the reason he said that the man on the throne was a phony, and he was the real king. What happened, he explained, was when he was a baby his royal nurse took her eyes off him as he lay in the yard, and he was attacked by a pig which bit off his ear. Fearful of the repercussions she swapped out the injured bairn with the baby of a local carter. Thus the 'true' king was raised in poverty and a low-born wretch was ruling England.

Now this may sound utterly absurd[66] but it speaks to the unpopularity of Edward at the time that rumours began to spread that maybe he wasn't the real king after all. John proposed a simple solution to the problem – he would fight Edward in single combat, and whoever won would take the throne. Edward was not particularly taken with this idea, and decided instead to have John arrested and tortured at which point he confessed that he had made the whole story up. Except it wasn't his fault! One day he had been walking across Christchurch Meadows with his pet cat (who he now realised was obviously the devil[67]) when it suggested the plan and convinced him to go through with it. The 'it wasn't my idea, the cat led me astray!' defence didn't do John any favours, and he was hanged. Just to be sure though (because this was medieval England) they, err, hanged his cat too.

Rumours abound that centuries of cat persecution in Europe ultimate came back to bite the humans who carried it out. It has been claimed that the reduced numbers of cats allowed rats and mice to flourish. The rats in particular were hosts for the fleas that carried the bubonic plague which ravaged the continent on multiple occasions from the 14th to 18th centuries. The evidence to back up this theory really doesn't exist though. It is *possible* that the demonisation of cats reduced their numbers sufficiently for there to be *slightly* high numbers of rats around, but the impact is likely to be trivial. Despite the church and various obsessed citizens taking issue with cats (and the people who lived with cats) there were still a hell of a lot of cats around. One reason we can be sure

---

[66] Because it was.

[67] Obviously.

of this is actually due to the outbreak of the Great Plague of London in 1665. In order to slow the spread of the disease, the mayor ordered the killing of all of the cats and the dogs in the city (as it was thought that they were, at least in part, responsible for transmitting it). This was an estimated total of 40,000 dogs and 200,000 cats. Given that the population of London at the time was around 460,000 people, that works out at more than one cat per household. To put this in context, there are thought to be 580,000 cats living in London today, with a human population of nearly 9 million people. There were a heck of a lot more cats per head of the population than there were 350 years ago even though we don't think that they are manifestations of the devil any more.[68]

Now you may be forgiven for thinking that I am perhaps exaggerating the disdain that medieval Europeans had for cats. Well, here is a little story that may just convince you otherwise. Please allow me to introduce Franz Helm of Cologne, who was an artillery master[69] in the first half of the 16th century. Helm was something of the Elon Musk of his day, except that his specialities weren't electric cars, rockets, or being opinionated on Twitter – rather, they were firing things at, and setting fire to, cities. Four hundred years ago there weren't really such things as artillery battles – two forces opposing each other on the opposite sides of a field and firing things at each other; no, artillery was used to overcome besieged cities. By smashing holes in their defences or setting them on fire.[70] Helm was an expert in this field, and in 1625 he published the influential *Armamentarium principale oder Kriegsmunition und Artillerie-Buch.*[71] In this tome he critically assessed all of the existing means of attacking cities (including

---

[68] I personally don't, that is. There may be some people who still think this. After all, take a population of 9 million people and you are pretty much sure to find at least one person who believes *anything* you can imagine, no matter how absurd.

[69] He was described as a 'shooter, cannonier and fireworker'. What is worth adding is that 'fireworker' didn't mean someone who shot pretty rockets into the sky on special occasions. No, it meant a person who is *really really good* at setting fire to stuff. Yes, that was a useful life skill in the 16th century.

[70] Or often both. At the same time.

[71] 'Principles of armament, or book of war munitions and artillery'.

many detailed in 1420's *Feuerwerkbuch*[72]) as well as suggesting a number of innovative means of attack.

If you are fond of cats, and are of a sensitive nature, you may wish to skip this part. In order to set fire to well-fortified cities that were impregnable to other forms of attack, Helm proposed the use of the 'rocket-cat'. Now you may think that is some kind of mistranslation, or misunderstanding. Surely he didn't proposing using cats with rockets attached to them? Nah. He did. He totally did. Don't believe us? Take a look at the picture here, which is taken from his gosh-darned actual book!

How did the 'rocket-cat' work? Helm usefully explains what to do in the text:

> Create a small sack like a fire-arrow… if you would like to get at a town or castle, seek to obtain a cat from that place. And bind the sack to the back of the cat, ignite it, let it glow well and thereafter let the cat go, so it runs to the nearest castle or town, and out of fear it thinks to hide itself where it ends up in barn hay or straw it will be ignited.

Thankfully there is no evidence that anyone ever actually followed Helm's advice. It has been pointed out that while you may be able to strap a load of burning stuff and explosives to the back of a cat you sure as hell can't control where they are going to run to. The poor, freaked-out animals are just going to go crazy and run in all directions. Quite possibly into your own camp, setting that on fire instead.

Well, at least more recent military minds don't have such bat-shit[73] crazy ideas about using wild animals as incendiary devices! Hold that thought, while I tell you another story. This one isn't about cats, it's

---

[72] 'Firework Book'. No, still not Roman candles or Catherine Wheels.

[73] Sorry in advance.

about bats.[74] During the Second World War the United States military came up with something called the 'bat-bomb'. The concept was simple. Take a hibernating Mexican free-tailed bat. Actually, take a *thousand* of them. Stick them into a large bomb casing. Oh, wait, before you do, attach a 14g (0.5 ounce) timed napalm incendiary bomb to each bat. Then drop the bat-bomb over Tokyo (where many houses were made of wood and paper). As these bomb wafted down on their parachutes the casings would spring open, releasing (and, presumably, rudely awakening) the bats. The bats (a little bleary eyed) would head to the nearest places to roost. The bombs would detonate, Tokyo would burn to the ground. Simple.

The man behind the bat-bomb was a dental surgeon named Lytle S. Adams[75] who believed that bats were created

> by God to await this hour to play their part in the scheme of free human existence, and to frustrate any attempt of those who dare desecrate our way of life.

President Theodore Roosevelt was well aware of this plan, and said of Adams: 'This man is not a nut. It sounds like a perfectly wild idea but is worth looking into.'[76]

This wasn't just some crazy theoretical exercise. The USA actually *built and tested* bat-bombs. In the first test the bats were accidentally released early and roosted under a fuel tank. Which they ignited. Incinerating the test range. Ultimately the project got canned because it was decided that nuclear weapons would be more effective.[77]

Sorry, I have taken you on a diversion into 20th century bat warfare. Let's get back to medieval Europan cats. In Tudor England there was also the tradition of, err, interring the body of an embalmed cat in the walls of a new house. The belief (seemingly) was that this would keep mice away from the house. I may be going

---

[74] Yes, I know that this is a book about cats, but this is just one story, and the word 'bat' is just a one-letter alphabetical step away from the word 'cat'.

[75] What does a dental surgeon know about warfare? Very little, it transpires.

[76] He thought this. He was President of the USA. Nonetheless the Allies won the war. Incredible.

[77] A good result for the bats. Perhaps not for humanity. Actually, we haven't done a thorough bat-casualty assessment of the attacks on Hiroshima and Nagasaki. It was probably a bad result for bats *as well*.

out on a limb here, but it does seem that the Tudors missed an important point about the whole cat-mouse interaction. It only works if you have a *living* cat to kill the mice. A dead one, particularly a dead one blocked up in your walls, is not going to be *any use at all.*

Just to warn you, this next bit is somewhat gruesome. Actually very gruesome. I found it very upsetting – please feel free to skip it. For hundreds of years, right up to the end of the 18th century, *cat burning* was a popular form of entertainment around midsummer, particularly in France and Belgium. Cats would be caught, imprisoned in sacks or wicker cages, and burned alive. These were not simply the pastimes of peasants. In 1648 Louis XIV himself lit a bonfire and danced in front of it as the cats became engulfed in flames. The American historian Robert Darnton wrote:

> Cats also figured in the cycle of Saint John the Baptist, which took place on June 24, at the time of summer solstice. Crowds made bonfires, jumped over them, danced around them, and threw into them objects with magical power, hoping to avoid disaster and obtain good fortune during the rest of the year. A favorite object was cats—cats tied up in bags, cats suspended from ropes, or cats burned at stake. Parisians liked to incinerate cats by the sackful, while the Courimauds (or 'cour à miaud' or cat chasers) of Saint Chamond preferred to chase a flaming cat through the streets. In parts of Burgundy and Lorraine they danced around a kind of burning May pole with a cat tied to it. In the Metz region they burned a dozen cats at a time in a basket on top of a bonfire. The ceremony took place with great pomp in Metz itself, until it was abolished in 1765...

There are some places in Europe where, thankfully, cats have been treated with the respect that they deserve for hundreds of years. In 1745 Queen Elizabeth of Russia ordered that cats be placed in the Hermitage Palace (it is now the Hermitage Museum) in Saint Petersburg in order to keep down the population of mice. Legend has it that these were not just ordinary moggies off the street; rather, they were shipped in from the city of Kazan which was noted for having cats that were excellent at catching mice. Apparently the queen ordered her minions:

to find in Kazan... the best and biggest cats capable of catching mice, and send them to... the Court of her Imperial Majesty, along with someone to look after and feed them, and send them by cart and with sufficient food immediately.

The cats thrived in the palace for almost 200 years, despite their home being stormed by the Bosheviks in 1917. Alas they all perished in during the siege of Leningrad during the Second World War, but after three catless years they were replaced. Today there are somewhere between 60 and 70 cats in the palace, looked after by three caretakers, with their own kitchen and even a small cat hospital. Their increasing fame (and cuteness) has caused them to become one of the main attractions in the palace, so much so that they even have their own dedicated press secretary.[78] Since 2011 the museum has held a 'catfest' to celebrate its cats with scavenger hunts and cat-painting competitions for children.[79]

Cats in the Americas

Domestic cats arrived in the Americas with the Europeans. There were a large number of wild cats, both large and small, but unlike in Asia and Africa it seems that they had not been domesticated. This could be due to the fact that the smaller cat species in South America were elusive jungle cats that had little exposure to humans, or that these species were simply not suited to domestication. The nature and development of agriculture could also have played a part. Hunter-gathering played a much more significant role in the continent than it did in Asia and North Africa at the time that cat domestication emerged. There was agriculture taking place, particularly of maize, but there would not have been the same scale of multi-year grain stores that were found in Egypt.[80]

The novelty of domestic cats to the indigenous people of the

---

[78] I had no idea that being a 'cat press secretary' was a possible career path. How do you get into it, do you think? Do you start with marketing for a bunch of kittens and work your way up?

[79] Painting pictures of cats, not actual cats, we assume. And, significantly, *no throwing cats off tall towers!* Take note, people of Ypres!

[80] More consistent harvests probably helped. The annual flooding of the Nile was super-important in ancient Egypt, and in a dry year people were pretty screwed.

Americas can be seen through how they were named. The Nuxalk people, an Indigenous First Nation who live around Bella Coola in what is today commonly called British Columbia, gave the Europeans who arrived in the 18th century the name *q'umsciwa*, a word that they also used to describe things that had returned from the dead (the pale skin of these arrivals apparently made them seem like ghosts). The name that the Nuxalk gave to the cats they brought with them was *q'umsciwaalhh*, which broadly translates as 'the thing that came with the *q'umsciwa*'. It is clear that they considered these small, friendly felines as being something very distinct from the larger wild cats that they were used to encountering. In many of the other First Nations languages, the word for a domestic cat is adopted or adapted from English of French. One exception is in Chinook Wawa, a pidgin trade language that used to be used by a range of different groups who lacked a common tongue. In Chinook Wana a domestic cat is called a *puspusii* or *puspus*, a name derived from their word for a cougar – *pus*. Is this why we refer to puss-cats today? No, as I will explain later similar names for cats emerged independently in a vast array of different languages around the world.

Cats in the Americas had similar problems to their European counterparts in the 17th century, as the craze for hunting down witches took place on both sides of the Atlantic. The most famous American case is, of course, the Salem Witch Trials which took place in New England between February 1692 and May 1693. A total of 30 people were found guilty; 19 of them were executed and five died in prison. Oh, and one man who refused to engage with the trial was pressed to death.[81]

---

[81] Do you really want to know what this entails? Okay. They lay you down and put a wooden board on top of you. They then pile stones on top of the board, with the expectation that the intense pain will cause you to cooperate. Sometimes they didn't bother with the board and just piled rocks on top of you. Giles Corey, the poor chap who experienced this at Salem, was the only American to die by this method (or at least die by this method applied by the authorities). It is thought that he refused to plead because he thought that by not doing so the authorities couldn't take his estate off him, and that whatever he did plead he would be found guilty and be executed, so better to die and safeguard his estate for his surviving family. Turns out this belief was wrong, and they took his estate. We have a lot a of time for old Giles it has to be said. It took him three days to die, and each time he was asked if he would make a

The first person to be accused of practicing witchcraft in the Salem witch trials was a woman named Tituba. She was a slave (hence no last name) and was believed to have originally come from South America, by way of Barbados. She, and two others, were accused of using witchcraft to harm two young girls. Under the pressure of questioning from the judge, John Hathorne she confessed, and spun a fanciful tale in which a red cat and a black cat told her to hurt the children. Amazingly, she survived the hangman's noose, but many others did not.

If you have seen (or heard) the musical *Hamilton* you may recall it being told that Martha Washington named one of her tomcats after Alexander Hamilton as both human and puss vigorously pursued the female members of their species. Indeed the character of Hamilton himself turns to the audience and says 'That's true!'. Um, well, actually it *isn't* true and there are a couple of reasons why. Firstly, there simply isn't any evidence that this was the case, but hey, absence of evidence isn't evidence of absence.[82] What is more compelling is the fact that George and Martha Washington didn't actually own any cats. They had *a lot* of dogs, and horses, and a donkey, and even a parrot, but no cats. Sure, there were probably some wandering out Mount Vernon, tormenting mice, but they were not creatures that had names appended to them. The book of the musical acknowledges that the whole Martha Washington thing isn't true, but goes on to suggest that the story was invented and spread around by John Adams as a means of smearing Hamilton's name. But, err, that isn't true either.

In case you are wondering the first presidential cat (see the 'Amazing Cats' chapter for more of them) arrived in the White House with Abraham Lincoln, the 16th President of the United States, who took office in 1861. I have to confess that I was a little disappointed that it took so long, particular as the following animals had already lived with previous presidents:

---

plea he simply said 'more weight'. Apparently those were his final words. Twenty years after his death he was formally absolved of any crime, so *that's all right then.* His wife, Martha, did plea, was found guilty, and executed. She was never absolved.

[82] I am quite fond of this saying.

- Dogs (many, many, dogs)
- Horses (again, loads of them)
- Donkeys
- Parrots
- Fighting cocks
- An alligator[83]
- Silkworms[84]
- Goats
- An eagle
- Two bear cubs
- Two tiger cubs[85]
- A mockingbird
- A canary
- Some white mice[86]

Lincoln's cats were named Tabby and Dixie and he was very devoted to them. Assistant Secretary of the Treasury Mansell B. Field wrote of him:

> He was fond of dumb animals, especially cats. I have seen him fondle one for an hour. Helplessness and suffering touched him when they appealed directly to his senses, or when you could penetrate through his intelligence to them.

I am not sure that Lincoln would have approved of the term 'dumb animals' though he would often pick up a cat and talk to it for as much as half an hour at a time and was once reported to have said:

> Dixie is smarter than my whole cabinet! And furthermore she doesn't talk back!

---

[83] It is said to have lived in the East Room of the White House for two months, under John Quincy Adams. This probably isn't actually true though.

[84] Pretty boring pets.

[85] They belonged to Martin Van Buren – they were a gift from the Sultan of Muscat and Oman. Congres forced him to give them to a zoo in the end. We guess they *were* the first presidential cats, but not the kind you could have curled up on your lap.

[86] There were not official presidential pets. Andrew Johnson, who had no official pets, apparently liked to feed a family of white mice who lived in his bedroom.

During the siege of Petersburg in 1865, Lincoln was visiting the headquarters of Ulysses S. Grant when he heard some kittens crying outside the tent. Admiral David Porter recounted that Lincoln was soon

tenderly caressing three stray kittens. It well illustrated the kindness of the man's disposition, and showed the childlike simplicity which was mingled with the grandeur of his nature.

As he stroked them Lincoln whispered to the kittens

Kitties, thank God you are cats, and can't understand this terrible strife that is going on.

Before leaving Lincoln made sure that the kittens would be cared for, telling a colonel:

I hope you will see that these poor little motherless waifs are given plenty of milk and treated kindly.[87]

---

[87] What a nice president!

Cats in Myths and Folklore

In the previous section I have already shared some of the myths and stories about cats, but these represent just a tiny fraction of the total. Given the lengthy of time cats have spent winding through the history of humanity, it is perhaps not surprising how often they appear in our folk tales.

Let's start by exploring the concept of cats and luck (or lack thereof). Black cats are generally considered to be unlucky both in general and particularly if one crosses your path.[88] This superstition probably arises from the whole 'black-devil-cat-bum-kissing' thing that I talked about in the section on witchcraft earlier. It could also some from Cat Sìth,[89] a fairy creature in Celtic mythology. Cat Sìth was a large black cat with a white spot on its chest and the beastie was not well liked by those who knew of it. In the Scottish Highlands people believed that it could steal a person's soul from their corpse before the gods claimed it. They believed this sufficiently strongly that teams of people would keep watch over a body between the point of death and burial in what was called the *Feill Fadalach*. Fires were forbidden during these watches as it was believed that they would attract warmth-seeking cats. Cats that

---

[88] I have always wondered what "crosses your path" means practically. Does it mean it crosses in front of you? If so, that isn't *yet* your path – you could turn and head a different way. It is more accurate in that case to say that, if you continue, that you have crossed the *cat's* path. Does it then mean that the cat crosses your path if it crosses the route you have already taken behind you? In either case, how near does this crossing need to happen? Do you have to *see* the cat in question? If a cat crossed a path you happen to be walking up five years earlier, does that count? Come on people! Establish some formal rules here!

[89] Is this where the name "Sith" comes from in the Star Wars Extended Bobbins Universe? Yes. Probably.

look like Cat Sìth also appear in an old British folk tale called 'The King of Cats':

> A man comes home to tell his wife and cat, Old Tom, that he saw nine black cats with white spots on their chests carrying a coffin with a crown on it, and one of the cats tells the man to 'Tell Tom Tildrum that Tim Toldrum is dead.' The cat then exclaims, 'What?! Old Tim dead! Then I'm the King o' the Cats!' Old Tom then climbs up the chimney and is never seen again!

You may think that such superstitions are relics of the ancient past, and that no one believes them today. There is some evidence to suggest that they do. In the UK the charity Cats Protection found that on average it took 13% longer to find a home for black rescue cats than for felines of other colours. Similar results have been found with cat rescue organisations in the USA as well. The problem of rehoming black cats had become so serious a 'Black Cat Day' has been created in the UK (27 October) and a 'Black Cat Appreciation Day' in the USA (17 August).[90] Black cats are not universally considered to be unlucky though. In Japan they are considered to be lucky, particularly for single women – it was thought that they were effective in attracting a high-quality husband! Eighteenth-century pirates believed, rather confusingly, that if a black cat walked towards someone they would have bad luck, but if it walked away from them then they would have good luck.[91] It was also thought that if a cat walked onto a ship, and then walked off it, then the ship was cursed to sink on its next voyage.[92]

In Latvia things are much clearer: black cats are lucky, as they can bring a good harvest for a farmer, particularly if the cat plays in the farmer's fields. It is thought that black cats are incarnations of the god of the harvest Rungis. In nearby Russia, however, cats are once more considered to be *bad* luck. If one crosses your path I have seen it said that you should walk backwards holding one of

---

[90] Um, why couldn't you all get together and have a single, global black cat day?

[91] No, I don't know what happens if a cat walks towards you and then walks away from you. Which is annoying because most of my encounters with cats involve them walking towards me, being fussed for a time, and then walking away from me.

[92] Again, it would be good to understand time-frames here. If a cat walks onto a ship it is pretty likely to walk off it again at some point. Eventually.

your shirt buttons to avoid misfortune. Or alternatively (this is actually a tale from Lithuania, but we think it is of Russian origin) you should spit three times over your left shoulder to escape the curse. If the cat was blue then things are quite different; blue cats are considered lucky in Russia.

The number of toes also can play a part in the luckiness of a cat. You may have come across a cat with extra toes at some point. We'll talk more about the biology of these *polydactyl cats* a little later – what matters for now is that they were considered to be particularly lucky by sailors. This is perhaps because the extra toes made them more efficient climbers (and hence mousers) aboard ships. As a result of this, many were brought over by settlers to North America and they are particularly prevalent in New England to this day. Their European cousins were not so fortunate. Additional toes were seen as signs of devilishness, and so polydactyl cats were *even more* likely to be killed than their regular-toed counterparts.[93]

Another superstition relating to cats (of all colours, not just black ones this time) is that they can *steal* the breath of a recently born baby and cause it to die. Not simply suffocate the poor bairn, no, actually *steal its breath*. The first reference in print to this phenomenon is believed to date from 1607 and it has been widely repeated since. It is fairly easy to see how this myth could have arisen. Cats like warm, comfortable places, and a baby's crib is likely to be just such a place. Sadly, young babies do sometimes die, seemingly inexplicably – something nowadays call *Sudden Infant Death Syndrome (SIDS)*. In less rationale times, if a baby were to be found dead without a mark on its body, and a cat sleeping in the crib, one can see how an erroneous conclusion could be drawn. The concept of specifically *stealing* the breath rather than simply *suffocating* a child could also have a (semi) rational basis. If a baby's face were smeared with milk then it is not beyond imagination that a cat may try and lick if off,[94] and this could appear to be breath-stealing in progress. In Plymouth, England in 1791 at a coroner's

---

[93] Sigh. Seriously, olden-times Europeans, give cats a break, you superstitious feline killers!

[94] Cats have licked all kinds of things off our fingers and faces. Writing that down makes it sound a bit gross. It didn't seem gross at the time(s). It seemed super-cute!

inquest a jury found that the cause of death of a child had been a cat sucking out its breath. Less than a hundred years ago, in 1929, a doctor[95] was quoted in the *Nebraska State Journal* that he had seen:

> the family pet in the very act of sucking a child's breath, lying on the baby's breast, a paw on either side of the babe's mouth, the cat's lips pressing those of the child and the infant's face pale as that of a corpse, its lips with the blueness of death.

In Iceland people weren't worried about cats killing babies, they were worried about cats killing *anyone*. Every year at Christmas a giant, vicious 'Yule Cat' named Jólakötturinn was said to stalk the land and devour people. He had a very specific criterion about which people he would eat though – only those who hadn't received new clothes on Christmas Eve were on the menu. The reason for this is thought to be a means of encouraging generosity – if people couldn't afford new clothes for themselves or their children, a gift from a friend or neighbour would save them from a brutal death.

Another giant cat that will also, err, eat you is Kot Bayun from Slavic folklore. He is huge, dark and fluffy and initially sounds like a friendly beast – he will wander up to you and tell you wonderful magical stories. Alas once these stories have lulled you to sleep he will eat you. A cat was also known to associate with Veles the god of the underworld, and as such death was thought to appear to people at the end of their lives in the form of a cat. If that person then did sadly die it was very important that a cat didn't jump over the body, as this would cause them to resurrect as a vampire. As the gatekeeper of the underworld, the cat was rejecting the person's soul through the act of jumping, cursing it to wander the earth for eternity.

Given that cats had these, let's be honest, not great associations in Slavic mythology it seems reasonable to think that they would have been as hated and persecuted as they were in other parts of medieval Europe. Actually, the opposite was true. Killing a cat was said to bring a person seven years of bad luck and abject misery, and so they were treated with considerable respect.

---

[95] Yes, this man said this and *he was allowed to practise medicine in the twentieth century!*

Many people today are probably more familiar with Puss in Boots from the *Shrek* films than the original folk tale, so it is probably worth retelling the story. The youngest son of a miller is disappointed to receive an inheritance that is only a *cat* – his eldest brother gets the mill, the middle brother gets the mules. This is, however, no ordinary cat. For starters, it can talk, and it asks the miller's son for a pair of boots. The young man provides them for the cat,[96] who proceeds to go out and hunt rabbits in the forest, presenting them to the king as presents from his master. One day the king is travelling through the land in a carriage with his daughter. The cat persuades his master to, err, take all of his clothes off. The cat then steals the clothes, and tells the king that his master, the 'Marquis of Carabas', has had his clothing stolen while swimming in the river. The king finds him a new set of awesome clothes[97] and gives the chap a lift, and his daughter immediately falls in love with him. The cat runs ahead and kills an ogre who happens to live in a nearby castle, so that when the king arrives there he believes that it belongs to the miller's son. The lad and the princess get married, and everyone lives happily ever after.[98]

The first European telling of this story in print dates from 16th century Italy, and numerous versions have appeared since. It seems likely though that original version of the story is *much* older than this. The *Panchatantra* is a collection of ancient Sanskrit animal fables dating from the second century BC and one of them tells a similar story of a cat trying to make his fortune from the king, although with considerably less success. The *Panchatantra* was widely circulated (translated into European languages) long before the Italian publication of *Puss in Boots* and it seems very likely that it influenced that tale. (Oh, and did you know that folklore has its own classification system, the Aarne-Thompson-Uther (ATU) system? *Puss in Boots* is classified at ATU545B, a subset of ATU545, 'The Cat as Helper' category.[99])

The Brothers Grimm also had a story about how a cat helped a

---

[96] This was probably a big expense for him; I'm not sure how he afforded it or *why* he went ahead and bought them. Still, the cat could talk...

[97] Did he just happen to have a set, in the correct size, in the carriage with him?

[98] Except the ogre who died, presumably unhappily.

[99] Well, *I* thought that was an interesting fact.

boy who worked for a miller, though this one was somewhat different. In this tale the miller (still alive) tells his three apprentices that he will give his mill to the one who can bring him back the best horse. The older two abandon the youngest, but not to worry! A cat appears and says words to the effect of 'If you work as my servant for seven years I will give you a totally amazing horse'. The boy obviously agrees and goes to work for the cat in a luxurious enchanted castle that is full of lovely cats. One would even dry his face with his tail. After seven years,[100] he returns, followed by a glorious horse *and* a magnificent carriage which contains a princess *who had been the cat all along.* He ends up marrying the princess, moving into the castle. Oh, and the miller gets to keep the horse.

While we are on the subject of cats helping young men make their fortune, it feels natural to talk next about Dick Whittington and his cat. The story that is normally told today has several different versions, and dates from the early 1600s. Although the precise details vary, the broad details are as follows. Dick Whittington, a poor country boy, comes to London to seek his fortune because he has heard that its streets are paved with gold. His cat follows him, which turns out to be a very good thing *indeed*. Or possibly he bought the cat for a penny that he earned from shining shoes, accounts vary. He is able to get a job as a kitchen boy in a rich merchant's house, paid in food and given a squalid attic room to live in. The room is full of mice and rats, but the cat handily takes care of the problem. The merchant – and this is where the story gets a little weird – arranges a trading expedition and persuades (or perhaps forces) Dick to add the cat to the cargo so that it might be sold abroad for profit.[101] Long story short, a Moorish king ends up buying the entire cargo of the ship for a massive amount of gold and holds a big banquet to celebrate. But wait! The banquet is overrun with rats and mice! Don't worry! The cat is there! The cat clears out the pests and the king is so pleased that he buys the cat for *ten times* the value of cargo of the ship.[102]

---

[100] The other two apprentices had also got horses, but they were (seemingly) sufficiently crap that the miller was happy to wait seven years on the off-chance that the third came back with a decent nag.

[101] Because obviously there are no cats in other countries.

[102] This does seem to be an unbelievable amount of money to pay for a cat. Oh, it

The ship returns, Dick gets stinking rich, marries his former master's daughter and becomes Lord Mayor of London.[103] The end.

WONDERFUL MUSEUM.

Portraits of Sr RICHᴰ WITTINGTON, & his Cat.
from an Original Painting at
MERCERS HALL.

The thing about the story of Dick Whittington is that it is based upon the life of a *real person* who lived from 1354 to 1423 and was actually Lord Mayor of London *four times*, as well as being a Member of Parliament and a Sheriff of London. The similarities with the folk tale pretty much disappear after that. He wasn't a poor country boy, he was born into an ancient and wealthy Gloucestershire family (his father was a knight and a Member of Parliament, and both of his elder brothers were also MPs). He was a hugely successful merchant (his sales to the king alone were more than £1 million in today's terms in just two years) and moneylender. There is no record at all

---

turns out that the cat is pregnant though.
[103] Not once. Not twice. But *three times*!

of him owning a cat.[104] What seems to have happened is that an older folk tale of a young man who made his fortune selling his cat abroad became merged with the story of Whittington's life around 150 years after his death. Cat or no cat, the legacy of Richard Whittington lives on to this day. Childless, he left his fortune to help the needy through the Charity of Sir Richard Whittington. As of 2020 the charity has more than £100 million in assets and spends around £3m a year housing and helping those in need.[105]

You will know by now the love and affection shown towards cats by the Japanese, so you may think that there are going to be lots of folk tales about sweet, wonderful and helpful cats. There are some, of course, but there are also quite a few about frankly terrifying cats. Stories of *nekomata* originated in China, but are most prevalent today in Japan. Nekomata are vast cat monsters that live in mountainous forests and, well, go around eating people. They are said to have originally been domestic cats who increased in size as they got old and, err, *grew a second tail*. As a result of this myth a folk belief developed in medieval Japan that cats should not be kept for too long lest they become nekomata and eat people up. One theory has it that this myth has an origin in truth, that at some point one or more man-eating tigers were on the loose in the Japanese woods, having been brought over from China and escaped from a menagerie. That doesn't really explain the whole two-tails thing though. Not all of these nekomata are evil, murderous monsters. One of them called *gotoku neko* usefully goes around stoking fires and breathing flames through a *hifukidake* – a bamboo blowpipe. Basically the gotoku neko wants to keep warm, so makes sure that hearth fires keep burning, even when people are not around. Oh, and it also wears a metal kettle stand on its head as a hat. I'm not really sure why.

A similar myth concerns the *bakeneko*, who are cats that if they are raised for seven years or longer will kill the human who looked after them. They only have one tail though. Some bakeneko were

<hr />

[104] Or indeed of a cat owning him. History just doesn't seem to have recorded this sort of stuff.

[105] I don't know about you, but I think that leaving a legacy that has helped people for *600 years* is pretty gosh-darned incredible!

said to be shape-shifters who took on human form, sometimes to, err, wear a towel on their head and start dancing (though in other stories they bewitched humans, had them slaughtered by wolves and were generally *not very nice*). It was also said that if a cat started licking the lamp oil then something odd would surely happen. Now you may think that a cat is pretty unlikely to lick lamp oil, until you learn that many people used fish oils, such as sardine oil, in their lamps because it was cheap – a tasty treat to a hungry cat. It is *possible* that this kind of behaviour inspired some of the cat-monster legends. A cat licking the oil from a lit lamp would have cast a large, dark shadow on the wall, perhaps making it seem like there was some kind of vast feline monster in the room. But for this to be true you would have to believe that the people in the room either hadn't noticed the cat licking on the lamp or simply had no idea how shadows work. Which seems pretty unlikely.

Finally in the pantheon of scary Japanese cat-spirits is the *kasha,* a hellish cat-demon whose favourite hobby is to steal the corpses of people (generally evil people) and then eat them. In the 1837 book *Hokuetu Seppu* ('Snow Stories of the North Etuse Province') the tale is told of the thwarting of a corpse-stealing kasha:

> It was in the Tenshō period. At a funeral in the Uonuma District, Echigo Province, a sudden gust and a ball of fire came flying to it, and covered the coffin. Inside the ball of fire, was a giant cat with two tails, and it attempted to steal the coffin. This yōkai was repelled by the priest of Dontōan, Kitataka, by his incantation and a single strike of his nyoi, and the kesa of Kitagawa was afterwards called the 'kasha-otoshi no kesa' (the kesa of the one who defeated a kasha).

In order to stop a kasha stealing corpses, a number of methods were employed in different parts of Japan. In Kamikuishiki a kasha was said to live nearby a particular temple. In order to prevent this flesh-feasting feline the priests would carry out a funeral twice. In the first one, instead of the body a rock was placed in the coffin to confuse the puss-cat. In Yawatahama a hair razor was put on top of the coffin to stop the cat getting inside. And in Misato before the funeral procession began, the words '*I will not let kasha feed on this*' were chanted twice.[106]

---

[106] In Japanese. Obviously.

Yet another evil cat monster is *El Broosha*. In Sephardic Jewish mythology this giant and, yes, yet again, black, cat-demon terrorises humans. El Broosha is specifically a *vampire-cat* that drains the blood of its victims and has a particular fondness for newborn babies. It is said that El Broosha is a manifestation of Lilith, Adam's first wife.[107]

Have you ever wondered why cats and dogs, well, fight like cats and dogs? An old Chinese folk tale has the answer. Once upon a time cat and a dog lived with a couple who owned a gold ring. Little did the couple know, but anyone possessing the ring would always be certain of having enough to live on. One day they sold the ring to get a little extra cash and their fortunes rapidly declined. They couldn't afford much food and the cat and the dog began to starve. The animals, who were friends at this point, came up with a plan to get the ring back. They knew (I don't know how they knew) it was being kept in a chest in a house on the other side of a river. So the cat caught a mouse, the mouse gnawed a hole in the chest, got the ring, and gave it to the cat.[108] The cat, holding the ring in its mouth, rode on the back of the dog as it swam back across the river. When the got to the other side they raced back home, but as the cat could climb over the houses that got in their way, and the dog had to run around them, the cat got back first.[109] The couple were thrilled that the cat had returned the ring and gave it a good fuss, a place by the fire and a saucer of milk. On the other hand they cursed and beat the dog, arriving shortly afterwards, for not trying

---

[107] Yup, Adam, as in 'Adam and Eve'. Eve was actually his second wife, his first was Lilith (according to some sources). She gets a mention in the Book of Isaiah: 'Her nobles shall be no more, nor shall kings be proclaimed there; all her princes are gone. Her castles shall be overgrown with thorns, her fortresses with thistles and briers. She shall become an abode for jackals and a haunt for ostriches. Wildcats shall meet with desert beasts, satyrs shall call to one another; There shall the Lilith repose, and find for herself a place to rest.'

[108] The story is unclear about what was in it for the mouse at this point. If we were a mouse that had been caught by a cat and gnawed a hole and got into a chest we would have *totally* stayed there until the cat had lost interest and wandered off.

[109] As this was rural China in the middle ages the houses can't have been so large that running around them would have made an appreciable difference in our opinion. Also climbing over something, even if you are an agile cat, doesn't seem to be much faster than going around it.

to get the ring back. And the dog has been the enemy of the cat ever since.

Another story involving cats and rings comes from ancient Siam (modern day Thailand). The background is a little convoluted, but in a nutshell, in order to keep their rings from being stolen a group of princesses threaded them on to the tail of a helpful cat. The cat was able to scamper around on rafters and roofs out of the reach of any thieving commoners, thus protecting the rings. Sadly for the cat, the weight of the rings was such that its tail buckled, leaving it crooked and that is why today all Siamese cats have crooked tails.

And finally, a cat myth from the Americas. Well, a cactus-cat myth to be exact. Yes, tales were told of large cat-shaped cacti in Pueblo and Navajo country. That could walk. And also liked to drink booze. Now because there was a distinct lack of bars and liquor stores in the middle of the desert, the ingenious cat would make its own. It would walk in a large circuit slashing at the base of giant cacti with its razor-sharp cat-cactus claws. This would cause the sweet, milky sap to seep out and ferment in the hot sun.[110] By the time it had slashed the 80th cactus the sap from the first would be sufficiently boozy to drink and so it would walk the circuit again, getting increasingly tipsy as the journey advanced. Wily locals, who were partial to a tipple themselves, would keep track of the cat and aim to get one cactus ahead of it so that they could guzzle the booze before it got there. But woe betide you if the cat caught up with you: you would get beaten to death with its spiny tail and your body would be covered with tiny red welts. People were found dead in the desert with just such injuries but there is likely a more rational explanation than an attack by an angry cat-plant. They almost certainly would have died from dehydration and/or heat exhaustion, and the marks on their body the signs of prickly heat. But hey, no one actually *saw* them die, so perhaps it was cactus-cat after all?

Further examples of cats in folklore can be found in Aesop's

---

[110] This might sound unlikely, but the Mexican drink *pulque* has been made for thousands of years from the sap of the large succulent maguey plant. The heart of a mature plant is cut out, and the sap starts to accumulate in the depression that is left. I can actually start fermenting right there, but it collected and put into vats to mature properly. The resulting drink is milky and tastes a little like sour yeast.

fables. These are said to have been written by a slave who is thought to have lived in ancient Greece between 620 and 564 BC. Fables are pithy little stories that aim to convey a particular moral message or lesson and typically contain animals (and other non-human things) acting like people. Quite a few of his tales involved cats and, generally speaking, they come across as devious, clever and cunning creatures.

Cats in Language

The Naming of Cats

Why do English speakers call cats 'cats'? Well, the modern English word 'cat' comes from the Old English word, um, *catt*. 'Catt' is thought to be derived from the Latin word *cattus,* which was first used at the start of the sixth century. Where did the Latin word come from? Ah. Well. That is where things start to get a bit complicated. It is possible that it came from an Egyptian word that developed into Coptic, ϣⲁⲩ (pronounced *šau*). It is also possible that the Arabic ﻗﻂ (pronounced *qatt*) was borrowed by the Nubians who turned it into *kaddîska*. It is also possible that the word originated from the Northern Sami people (who live in northern Norway, Sweden and Finland) and then moved to ancient German, and then to Latin, and then to Greek, and then to Syriac and Arabic. All of which is a long-winded way of saying that we really don't know for sure. At all.

The English term puss[III] *used* to describe a cat has been around for about 500 years and probably either came from the Dutch *poes* or the Low German *puuskatte*. As I mentioned earlier it is fascinating that at the same time, thousands of miles away, the word *pus* was used in Chinook Wana as the word for a cougar and that this arose totally independently. Again, no one is really sure how the word arose, but it has been suggested that it simply developed from the sound people made to attract cats. But that theory can't really explain it all. I can't imagine anyone calling out 'here puss puss' to a wild cougar...

You probably know that an unneutered male cat is called a *tom*,

---

[III] Promise fulfilled (see earlier).

but did you know that an unspayed female cat is called a *queen*? Or that a neutered male cat is called a *gib*? We all know that young cats are called kittens, but they also used to be called *catlings*. Finally, the correct term for a group of cats is either a *glaring* (I totally get that) or a *clowder*[112] (I literally have no idea). Okay. I *had* no idea, but I looked it up. It seems that the word *clowder* evolved from the word *clodder* which, 250 years ago, meant 'a clotted mass'. I guess I can see how a big group of cats together could look a *bit* like a 'clotted mass' but frankly I think that *glaring* is a much, much better word.

A clowder of cats

Words for 'cat' in different languages generally fall into one of three categories (no pun intended).

Firstly, words that sound something like 'cat' such as:
- Arabic – qut (cut)
- Armenian – katu
- Basque – katu
- Bulgarian – kotka
- Czech – kocka

---

[112] Yes, this made me think initially that this was some weird truncation of 'clam chowder'. Is isn't though.

- Dutch – kat
- Filipino – cat
- French – chat
- German – katti, katze or ke
- Greek – gata
- Hebrew – chatul or kats
- Icelandic – kottu
- Lithuanian – katinas
- Portuguese – gato
- Russian – kot (male cat)
- Spanish – gato
- Swedish – katt
- Zulu – ikati

Then there are words that sound something like 'puss':
- Dutch – puse (as well as kat)
- Filipino – pusa (as well as cat)

And finally words that sound a bit like 'miaow':
- Mandarin Chinese – miu or mau
- Thai – Mæw
- Vietnamese – meo
- Egyptian – 𓏎𓏏𓅱𓃠 miw

The term 'moggie' or 'moggy' or simple just 'mog' is often used in the UK to refer to a cat – generally a regular, non-pedigree type of beastie. It isn't clear exactly how this term arose, possibly it came from the shortening of the name Margaret to *Maggie* but, err, it is yet another cat linguistic mystery.

Cat-related Idioms

Probably because cats have been such an important part of our lives for so long numerous phrases have crept into the English language that make reference to them. Sometimes confusingly so:

Sourpuss

Let's start with an expression that actually has nothing to do with cats! *Sourpuss* meaning someone who is grumpy actually comes from the use of the word *puss* as a slang term for 'mouth' – so, a sour mouth.

Like the cat that got the cream

A cat who has got the cream is going to be a very happy cat indeed, and so this expression is used to describe someone who is feeling rather self-satisfied, possibly to the point of smugness. *The cat who got the canary* is a more American version of the same expression.

Cat-o'-nine-tails

The cat o' nine tails (commonly referred to as 'the cat') is a highly unpleasant device that was used to inflict physical punishment upon luckless victims, particularly in the British Royal Navy and Army. It is essentially a whip with a handle that is divided into nine thinner lengths at the end. This may not sound too bad, but these strands would slice through the naked skin of the victim's back creating a patchwork of lacerations. In the Royal Navy a dozen lashes might be given for a fairly minor offence such as drunkenness; more serious ones would call for upwards of a hundred which could result in death through blood loss or later infection. The threads were said to be akin to the claws of a cat due to the way that they would make parallel wounds in the flesh, and hence its name.

Not enough room to swing a cat

If you are in a small space you may say that there is 'not enough room to swing a cat'. It is often said that the phrase originates from the use of the cat o' nine tails mentioned above, particularly that in the confined spaces aboard ship there was not enough room to carry out a punishment beating. There isn't however any real evidence that this is the case. Indeed the 'swing a cat' phrase was recorded in print before the first known reference to the lash. Richard Kephale wrote in *Medela Pestilentiae* in 1665:

> They had not space enough (according to the vulgar saying) to swing a Cat in.

– suggesting that the expression was already in common use. It wasn't until 30 years later that we find the first reference to 'the cat' in William Congreve's *Love for Love*:

> If you should give such language at sea, you'd have a cat-o'-nine-tails laid cross your shoulders.

This therefore suggests, unhappily, that the phrase arose from the notion of grabbing a cat by the tail and swinging it around. Of course that this may not have been a thing people actually did, it could have just been a figure of speech, but given the medieval European attitudes towards cats I wouldn't want to bet on it.

Raining cats and dogs

If it is absolutely *tipping it down*,[113] it is *raining cats and dogs*. A very familiar expression, but if you think about it for more than a moment a really odd one. Why cats and dogs? They are not noted measures of volume nor do they tend to fall from the sky. You will be amazed to learn that no one knows where the phrase originated. In 1651 the British poet Henry Vaughan wrote 'cats and dogs rained in a shower', the first known usage of the phrase in print, but it was Jonathan Swift who popularised the expression in the following century. One explanation I have come across is that the concept originated in ancient China when heavy storms would flood the gutters and wash the corpses of dead feral dogs and cats down the street. Another is that it comes from the Greek expression *cata doxa* meaning something that is hard to believe – hence if it is raining astonishingly hard it is raining *catadoxa*.[114] Or maybe it came from the Old English word *catadupe* meaning 'waterfall'? I thought that

---

[113] As I type these words it really is!

[114] Cute theory. Fits nicely. I don't believe it for a second.

it might be fun to come up with my own theory to see if I could get people to believe it. The rumble of thunder and this hissing of fast-falling rain sounds very much like the barking of dogs and the hissing of cats when they fight each other, and it was thought that god-like versions of these beasts were battling in the clouds during heavy thunderstorms. And so it became said that it was 'raining like cats and dogs'.[115]

Look what the cat dragged in

If you are looking dishevelled, unkempt, bedraggled, or even possibly a little the worse for wear from the previous night someone might say (a little rudely), 'Oh, look what the cat dragged in!' The expression has been around since about 1900 and it is one where the origin is pretty clear. Cats, as you well know, sometimes like to bring in dead prey, and this is simply comparing the subject of the expression to a mauled mouse. Or bird. Or vole. Or bat. Or... oh, you get the drift.

Not a cat in Hell's chance

If the odds are sufficiently stacked against you then it is often said you have about as much chance of a cat in Hell. The original version of this phrase clearly specified that it wasn't just the chance of a regular cat, but specifically one *without claws*.[116] The first reference to the phrase in print (though it was doubtless much older) comes from the *Oxford Journal* on 29 September 1753. It concerns the trial and execution of one John Billingsgate in Oxford[117] for crimes including 'scandal', 'abuse' and 'swearing'.[118] His punishment included having his tongue ripped out with red-hot pincers before the hanging itself. As the *Journal* tells it:

> Poor John Billingsgate the late Object of Publick Justice, is now a deplorable Spectacle, which by the singular and uncommon Circumstances attending his Condition, draws the Attention of all

---

[115] Frankly I think that this is about as credible as the other theories. For the record it was invented at 13:20 UTC on 31 October, 2020.

[116] This perhaps suggests that a cat *with claws* might be able to clamber up and escape from Hell?

[117] His execution took place around half a mile from where I am writing these words!

[118] These may not sound too bad, but he did actually murder someone.

the Civilians, Cockfighters, and Anatomists of this Place. Since his Tongue was cut out he has had no rest Day or Night [...]. When his Phrenzy is highest, he makes Signs for Pen, Ink and Paper; but these are now denied him, for the Experiment was made whether Writing would give him any Relief; and it was found that it was only adding Fuel to the Flame. The only intelligible Sentence he has wrote, is the following: 'Without a Tongue I have no more chance in Life, than a Cat in Hell without Claws.' Then he grew quite delirious.[119]

Apparently he took his fate fairly stoically, not swearing more than a dozen times in the time it took to take him from his house to the place of his execution.

Put (or throw) the cat among the pigeons

If you do or say something that causes a rumpus, then you have well and truly put the cat among the pigeons. The expression makes obvious sense: put a cat together with a bunch of pigeons and chaos is sure to ensure. But the combination of cat and pigeons seems a little odd. Surely people didn't put cats and pigeons together to see what would happen? If you have read this far in the book[120] then actually you probably *won't* be surprised that they did. It seems that the English in colonial India would think it fine entertainment to put a wild cat in a pen of pigeons and bet upon how many it would kill. The Dutch have a similar (but frankly weirder) proverb '*De knuppel in het hoenderhok gooien*', which translates to '*Throwing the bat into the chicken shed*'. The French version (thankfully) involves no animal cruelty whatsoever: '*Lancer un pavé dans la mare*' ('*Throwing a cobblestone in the pond*').

Let the cat out of the bag

If you have revealed something that you shouldn't have then you *let the cat out the bag*. Why do people say this? Um, no one knows. There is a theory that it relates to the expression 'a pig in a poke' meaning a thing that has been bought without being inspected, specifically someone thinks that they have just bought a little piglet

---

[119] Unsurprisingly.

[120] It would be a bit weird for you to be reading this if you haven't, unless you randomly opened it at this page.

at a market but upon opening their bag when they get home they find it is a cat instead.[121] In both French and Dutch the phrases for this scam make the feline element of it clear (*acheter (un) chat en poche* and *een kat in de zak kopen* respectively), translating as 'to buy a cat in a bag'. Opening the bag, and hence discovering the cat, seems like a sensible origin for the phrases, but there simply isn't the evidence to support it.

Cat got your tongue?

This means that you are unable (or unwilling) to speak and it *possibly* dates from the whole cats being associated with witches thing – a witch's cat would immobilise, or even physically steal, your tongue to keep you from speaking. There is a (frankly much more unlikely) theory that in ancient Egypt criminals would have their tongues cut out and fed to cats.

More than one way to skin a cat

If there are a number of different ways to do something then you could say that there is more than one way to skin a cat. This may sound as though it is a very old expression, however the first usage of it known only dates from the mid-19th century. It is likely to be a version of an earlier saying – *'there are more ways to kill a dog than hanging'*[122] – which dates from the 17th century. It was, depressingly, the case that in the 19th century cats were bred and killed for their fur, and even more depressingly, this practice continues in some parts of the world today.

---

[121] Okay, so I have a problem with the whole 'pig in a poke' thing. You see someone with a load of pigs at a market and say 'One pig please!' and the pig-seller says 'Of course, I happen to have one bagged up already, please take this one!' – are you really just going to hand over your cash and *not check the bag*? Also, pigs and cats have very different body shapes and let's face it a cat shut up in a bag is going to make its displeasure clearly known and it won't sound like oinking! Also, if this was supposed to be so commonplace that *there was a special expression for it*. Surely after it happened once or twice word would swiftly get around and everyone would be checking their pig-bags? There is something very fishy going on here.

[122] Really not sure why both of these phrases should involve doing nasty things to animals...

The cat's pajamas

If something is really excellent, it can be said to be 'the cat's pajamas' (US spelling). This, let's face it, very *odd* expression (as cats are not known to wear pajamas and they would likely be very annoyed to be put into them) is of unclear origin. It was certainly in use in the USA in the 1920s among the flapper set. Possibly the earliest reference in print comes from South Carolina's *The Pageland Journal* in 1918 – '*Wouldn't that beat the cat's pajamas?*'. The fact that the phrase was well known is shown by the fact that a New York woman dressed her cats up in pajamas[123] a few years later. As the *New York Times* reported on 6 November 1922:

> Sunday afternoon strollers in lower Fifth Avenue were treated to the unusual sight yesterday of a young woman clad in transparent yellow silk pajamas, escorted by four cats, also clad in pajamas, leisurely making her way along the avenue...

The phrase *the cat's whiskers*, meaning the same, originated at around the same time, as did *the cat's miaow.* Some people believe that the cartoonist and sportswriter Thomas Aloysuis Dorgan[124] (better known as Tad Dorgan) invented the phrases *the cat's miaow* and *the cat's pajamas*. Whether or not he did actually come up with them he did play a significant role in popularising them. Oh, and he is also said to have originated the expressions *hardboiled, for crying out loud!, dumbbell,* and the phrase *Yes, we have no bananas.*

Like herding cats

If you are trying to corral a group of wilful, independently minded people into acting as a group or agreeing to the same thing it can be very much like trying to herd cats. The origins of this phrase are pretty obvious – trying to get just one cat to do the thing that you want is nigh-on impossible. Trying to get a group of them to do the same is pure fantasy. This is probably the most recent cat-related expression as it appears to have originated in the IT industry in the USA in the early 1980s.

---

[123] Poor cats.

[124] That he became a hugely successful cartoonist is pretty incredible given that he lost all of the fingers off his right hand in a childhood accident.

Fat cat

Let's face it, cats can look a little, well, *smug* and fat ones particularly so. The phrase 'fat cat' arose in the 1920s to describe wealthy political donors who would use their cash to buy power, status and influence, oftentimes enriching themselves even further in the process. Today the term has expanded to include corporate executives and pretty much anyone who has an obscene level of wealth. The original fat cats were primarily men, of the stouter variety. As Frank Kent wrote in the *Baltimore Sun:*

A Fat Cat is a man of large means and slight political experience who, having reached middle age, and success in business, and finding no further thrill, sense or satisfaction in the mere piling up of more millions, develops a yearning for some sort of public honor, and is willing to pay for it. There are such men in all the States, and they are as welcome to the organization [i.e., the party] as the flowers in May. They relieve the pressure all along the line, lighten the load, make life brighter and better for the busy machine workers. The [political] machine has what the Fat Cat wants [i.e., public honor], and the Fat Cat has what the machine must have, to wit, money.

The nine lives of a cat

Cats do seem to have the habits of both getting themselves into precarious and dangerous situations and also getting out of them more or less unharmed. Their curiosity, climbing ability and flexibility will lead to them squeezing into tiny spaces and high up on tiny ledges and yet these same skills (and their ability to often survive great falls by landing on their feet) mean that they can usually escape from them. Although cats are said to have nine lives in many countries, differences of opinion do exist. In Italy, Germany, Greece, and Brazil they are said to have seven lives, and in Turkish and Arabic countries only six. One old English proverb suggests that these lives reflect the stages of a cat's life:

A cat has nine lives. For three he plays, for three is strays, and for the last three he stays.[125]

---

[125] It does rhyme nicely, but even elderly cats like to play!

Curiosity killed the cat

Cats are curious creatures, so it does make some kind of sense that scrabbling around in places that are dangerous could have had fatal consequences for them, and as such the phrase acts as a (somewhat pointed) warning for others to not be too inquisitive. The interesting thing though is that the expression in use today was didn't start out like that. Originally the phrase was '*Care will kill the cat*' or '*Care killed the cat*' – care in this context meaning worry or sorrow for others. In other words, too much concern for others could end up being damaging.

The earliest known usage of the phrase in print was by Ben Jonson in his 1598 play *Every Man in His Humour*:

> Helter skelter, hang sorrow, care will kill a cat, up-tails all, and a pox on the hangman.

William Shakespeare used the expression a year later in his play *Much Ado About Nothing* (he almost certainly appeared in the first production of Johnson's play):[126]

> What, courage man! what though care killed a cat, thou hast mettle enough in thee to kill care.

A slightly longer version of the saying was recorded at the end of the 19th century:

> Care killed the Cat. It is said that 'a cat has nine lives,' yet care would wear them all out.

It isn't clear when 'care' became 'curiosity' but it had definitely happened by 1868 when an Irish newspaper noted '*they say that curiosity killed a cat once*'. While you are probably familiar with this phrasing, you may not have known that there is a longer version of it too – one that has a better outcome for the cat: *Curiosity killed the cat, but satisfaction brought it back*. This flips the meaning on its head somewhat – the risk of inquisitiveness is offset by the value of the knowledge acquired. So, should anyone try to temper your curiosity with the phrase in the future, I hope that you considered replying 'but satisfaction brought it back'.

---

[126] Could Shakespeare have *stolen* the line? Let's just say that he might have *borrowed* it.

Domestic Cats Today

There are thought to be around 600 million domestic cats in the world today, though if you have read this far you probably won't be surprised to know that the precise[127] number is unknown. Of these more than 90 million live in the USA and 7 million in the UK. They are the most popular 'pet'[128] in the world, but there are actually more dogs in total, possibly as many as a billion of them, but many more of these are feral. Speaking of 'feral' it is probably worth explaining the three categories of domestic cat:

House cats are cats that live with humans. Some will spend their time between the inside and the outside, while others (indoor cats) will remain inside the property. Interestingly there are huge differences between countries in the proportion of cats that are indoor only as opposed to those allowed to venture outside. In Europe only around 10% of cats are indoor only, the remaining 90% being able to trot around in the fresh air. In the USA the position is almost completely the opposite, with around 90% of cats being indoor only. The American preference for keeping cats inside is partly due to a desire to protect them from diseases such as feline immunodeficiency virus (FIV) and to keep them safe from other dangers such as being hit by cars. If a cat has lived inside its whole life then it *probably* isn't missing being outside too much, but the keeping of cats totally inside does seem a little strange from the other side of the Atlantic. Interestingly, indoor-only cats only really started to exist in significant numbers in the 1950s thanks to the invention of cat litter.

---

[127] To be honest, even a *vague* number.

[128] I am not that keen on the word 'pet' but also think that 'companion animal' is a bit clunky.

Feral cats are 'unowned' cats that live wholly outside and generally avoid human contact as much as possible. There is something of a grey area between cats who might have once lived with humans and have, for whatever reason, become stray and those who were born and live totally outside without any human interaction. The number of feral cats in the world is even harder to pin down than the number of domestic cats – there are thought to be somewhere between 25 million and 60 million in the USA alone. While the closest wild relatives of the domestic cat, such as the European wildcat, will live solitary lives, feral cats will often form large colonies, particularly in areas where there are good sources of food. Around 200 cats live in the Colosseum in Rome for example, and are actually fairly happy and healthy. A group of women called *le gattare*, or 'the cat ladies', bring them and some of the other 300,000 feral cats in Rome food each day.

Farm cats are perhaps most easily described as being halfway between house cats and feral cats. They will live in and around barns and other agricultural buildings and keep down the rodent populations. Their diets will be sometimes supplemented by grateful farmers and they may even wander in and out of houses and allowed themselves to be petted by humans. Farm cats are probably the closest thing we have today to the earliest relationships between cats and humans that formed all those thousands of years ago.

House cats who are allowed to go outside often do so through a cat flap. The 'flap' part of the cat flap is a relatively modern addition; however, the concept of cutting a special hole to allow a cat to go into and out of barns and other buildings dates back to ancient Egypt. In the 'Miller's Tale' written by Geoffrey Chaucer a servant uses just such a cat-hole to peer into a house when no one answers his knocks at the door:

An hole he foond, ful lowe upon a bord
Ther as the cat was wont in for to crepe,
And at the hole he looked in ful depe,
And at the last he hadde of hym a sighte.

You may have heard it said that Sir Isaac Newton, discoverer of gravity, was the inventor of the cat flap. We can be sure that he didn't actually invent a cat flap, or indeed the notion of cutting a hole in a door for a cat to pass through, but the story is interesting nonetheless. When living in Trinity College, Cambridge, Newton owned a cat who went on to have kittens. To enable the mother cat to get in and out he cut a large hole in his door, and in order to create an entrance for the kittens he cut a smaller hole – not realising that they too could, obviously, use the larger hole. It doesn't quite seem to ring true that one of the greatest minds in history could make such an oversight and so the story has been long dismissed. However, a fellow of the same college did report in 1827:

> 'Whether this account be true or false, indisputably true is it that there are in the door to this day two plugged holes of the proper dimensions for the respective egresses of cat and kitten.

Given that Newton had been dead for more than 120 years by this point this isn't exactly compelling evidence, but hey, you never know. Until very recently cat flaps were fairly straightforward items, a swing door that your cat could push through without too much effort. Of course if it is easy for *your* cat to make its way in and out then it is also easy for *other* cats to do the same, leading to food thefts, cat fights, and sometimes unpleasant smells. Originally this problem was solved by getting the cat to wear a special collar that would enable only it to get through the flap. Collars can be very problematic however, not least because they can be easily lost, so today you can buy smart cat flaps that identify your cat from its embedded microchip. For those people who wanted to glam up their cat doorway, options are available. Possibly the most expensive (and absurd) was the $1,500 crystal-studded cat flap launched by Swarovski in 2009. I am pretty sure that any cats using it would have been deeply unimpressed by this addition of bling.

If you live with cats you know that your most important role – even above opening doors for those who don't have access to a cat flap – is providing them with food. It may come as something of a surprise to learn that it is only in the last 200 (out of the 10,000) years that we have been living together that the idea of feeding cats properly has developed. Until the early 19th century it was broadly assumed that cats could happily fend for themselves (unlike dogs who, lacking the same hunting opportunities, had been fed by humans for millennia). Indeed it was thought that by feeding your cat you would likely reduce its incentive to hunt and thereby reduce its efficacy as a pest-control device. In 1837 the French writer Mauny de Mornay challenged this view:

> It is... thought wrongly that the cat, ill-fed, hunts better and takes more mice; this too is a grave error. The cat who is not given food is feeble and sickly; as soon as he has bitten into a mouse, he lies down to rest and sleep; while well fed, he is wide awake and satisfies his natural taste in chasing all that belongs to the rat family.

The notion that a hungry cat would lie down to rest after biting into a mouse is perhaps a *little* bit off the mark, but the suggestion that even well-fed cats will hunt simply for amusement value certainly rings true – as anyone who has had a 'present' brought to them by their cat can attest.

The theory that a well-fed cat is a better hunter was share by his countryman Nicolas Jean-Baptiste, who wrote in 1844:

> Normally in the country no care is taken of a cat's food, and he is left to live, it is said, from his hunting, but when he is hungry, he hunts the pantry's provisions far more than the mouse; because he does not pursue them and never watches them by need, but by instinct and attraction. And so, to neglect feeding a cat, is to render him at the same time useless and harmful, while with a few scraps regularly and properly given, the cat will never do any damage, and will render much service.

By 1876 the writer Gordon Stables was giving specific advice about the best things to feed cats, along with some, shall we say, *unusual* suggestions about how to ensure that they keep themselves clean:

> If then, only for the sake of making (a cat) more valuable as a vermin-killer, she ought to have regular and sufficient food. A cat ought to be fed at least twice a day. Let her have a dish to herself, put down to

her, and removed when the meal is finished. Experience is the best teacher as regards the quantity of a cat's food, and in quality let it be varied. Oatmeal porridge and milk, or white bread steeped in warm milk, to which a little sugar has been added, are both excellent breakfasts for puss; and for dinner she must have an allowance of flesh. Boiled lights are better for her than horse-meat, and occasionally let her have fish. Teach your cat to wait patiently till she is served—a spoiled cat is nearly as disagreeable as a spoiled child. If you want to have your cat nice and clean, treat her now and then to a square inch of fresh butter. It not only acts as a gentle laxative, but, the grease, combining in her mouth, with the alkalinity of her saliva, forms a kind of natural cat-soap, and you will see she will immediately commence washing herself, and become beautifully clean. (N.B.—If you wish to have a cat nicely done up for showing, touch her all over with a sponge dipped in fresh cream, when she licks herself the effect is wonderful.) Remember that too much flesh-meat, especially liver,— which ought only to be given occasionally,—is very apt to induce a troublesome diarrhoea (looseness). Do not give your pet too many tit-bits at table; but whatever else you give her, never neglect to let her have her two regular meals.

Okay, so there is quite a lot to unpack in here. First off, as I shall discuss in more detail later, cats are *obligate carnivores* – meat needs to be a significant portion of their diet, so a breakfast of oatmeal is not going to be a great feast for them. Also most cats are lactose intolerant, so giving them untreated cow's milk is not ideal. Then there is the fact that due to a genetic mutation cats can't detect sweet tastes, so the addition of sugar would make no difference to them at all. Have no doubt about it, cats *love* butter and cream but, thanks to millions of years of evolution, have developed to become perfect self-cleaners without the addition of dairy products. Indeed, there is an old myth that when you bring a cat into a new home the best thing to do is to put butter on its paws. The belief was that, through washing, it would spread the butter all over its body and then be occupied for hours as it tried to clean it all off, by which time it would feel at home. As with most myths though it turns out that cats are actually very good at getting butter off their fur and so this would merely be a temporary diversion. While the cat is probably not going to like it, I do love the idea of sponging cream over a cat, not least because you could call out to your partner, 'Darling! I'm just off to cover the cat with cream!'

Teaching your cat to wait patiently until it is served is *excellent* advice but in my experience is a lot more easily said than done. The first specialist dog food arrived in 1860, manufactured by Spratt[129] of London and was followed a few years late by a cat-specific product. Prior to that it was traditional to feed cats horse meat (sorry horses) and dedicated vendors known as *cats' meat men* would sell it from barrows around towns and cities. Those barrow-pushing men would have a hell of a job meeting the cat food demands of today – in 2019 the global cat food market was valued at over $30 billion. That is a whole heap of food, and some people have understandably questioned the environmental impact of keeping pets. It has been estimated that around 2.5 *million* tonnes of fish alone are used in the production of cat food each year. That compares to around 160 million tonnes eaten each year by humans; however relatively speaking, cats eat a lot more fish per head than we do. To put the overall food needs of cats in some context, it has been calculated that the caloric consumption of cats in the USA is equivalent to that of around 200,000 humans, or 0.07% of the population.

We have already touched upon another environmental impact of cats – the prey animals that they kill. It is pretty clear in places such as Australia and New Zealand that had no native cat species our feline friends have caused some pretty serious depopulations for the local wildlife. But what about in countries that already had cats living there? Are domestic cats causing significant problems? The short answer is 'yes'. The longer answer is 'it's complicated'. An article published in 2013 in the scientific journal *Nature* estimated that domestic cats in the USA killed between 1.3 and 4.0 *billion* birds each year and an incredible 6.3–22.3 *billion* mammals such as mice and rats. It was concluded that domestic cats were the single greatest cause of human-related (through our introduction and support of

---

[129] Fun Spratt fact! Spratt provided dog biscuits to the British Army in World War I and kept meticulous records, down to the individual number of biscuits supplied – 1,256,976,708 – yup, over *one billion* dog biscuits.

cats) bird deaths is the country. That seems very cut and dried, so where is the complexity? Well, for starters the vast majority of these killings were not carried out by house cats (remember the vast majority of house cats in the USA do not venture outside at all). Rather, the large feral cat population that relies upon hunting for survival is the cause of the deaths. You may live with an outdoor cat who brings in the odd mouse, but their feral counterparts are each likely to make 100 times as many kills in a year. One then needs to take into account the fact that many of these prey animals would have died from other causes had they evaded the cats. In the UK the Royal Society for the Protection of Birds has estimated that domestic cats kill around 27 million birds each spring and summer. However, they note that there is evidence to suggest that the birds killed tend to be weaker or more elderly; and that relatively few of the chicks that are hatched each year survive to maturity the following year due to illness, starvation and other forms of predation. The bird species in the UK that have suffered the most significant declines in recent years (such as skylarks and corn buntings) live in rural areas with very few cats. Changes in agriculture and land use appear to be the key drivers in the reduction of their numbers.

It seems then that house cats themselves are not likely to be having a huge impact upon the populations of wild birds, but nonetheless it can be upsetting to see them kill just one. Putting a bell on a cat's collar does seem to make a difference, with some studies suggesting that it can reduce the number of animals that they kill by up to 50%. More recently different bird-protecting measures have been developed. 'Birdbesafe' make brightly coloured covers to go on a cat's collar – one study found that it reduced the number of birds killed by over 85%.[130] A more technical solution is a sonic collar which emits a loud screech when it senses the movement of the cat pouncing, giving the intended victim a few precious moments of extra warning to escape. Please remember though, if you do put a collar on a cat make sure that it is of the quick-release variety. Old-fashioned collars can cause horrendous injuries to cats and sometimes even kill them if they become trapped.

---

[130] If you look at pictures of cats wearing these colourful collar covers they look very displeased about the indignity of the situation.

Breeds of Cats

You probably have a reasonable idea of what a 'breed of cat' is – it is a type of cat that has a distinct, consistent set of physical characters which can be easily recognised. You may be wondering what the scientific definition of a 'cat breed' is, though. If so, you are going to have to continue wondering because there isn't one. Cat breeds do not have an objective or biologically verifiable classification; rather, a group of breeders reaches a consensus about what characteristics a breed has and creates a set of rules to either include or exclude cats from that category. To confuse things further, there is not a global consensus among cat breeders as to what a breed is, or even how many there are. The International Cat Association (TICA) recognises 71 standardised breeds. The Cat Fanciers Association, in contrast, a mere 44. This means that the same cat could be classified as one breed by one organisation and a different one by the other.

Is a cat of a specific breed a 'pedigree' cat? Not necessarily. A pedigree cat is basically a member of a cat breed that has good paperwork. Specifically paperwork showing the ancestry of the cat, usually going back three or four generations, that demonstrates that it is part of the breed. Around 10% of UK cats and 15% of USA cats are pedigree cats. There will be more cats that can be classified as being a specific breed, but still the majority of cats are breedless 'mongrels', a mash-up of different breeds. They are normally categorised as being 'domestic short-haired' or 'domestic long-haired' but these are simply descriptive terms based upon, you guessed it, the length of their fur. Because pedigree cats are bred from smaller gene pools than everyday moggies, there is a heightened risk of genetic disorders being spread down the generations. One example of this is polycystic kidney disease (PKD), which can often cause suffering and premature death in the cats that have it. It used to be the case that, due to inbreeding, as many as 50% of Persian cats were affected by PKD. Recently however breeders have been able to genetically test their cats, and prevent those carrying PKD from breeding.

As there are, well, somewhere between 44 and 71 breeds of cats I am not going to list them all, but I would like to share a couple of my favourites with you (though I should add at this point that the only cats I have ever lived with have been good old basic moggies).

Durator

The **Norwegian forest cat** (above) is, you will be amazed to learn, a breed commonly found in Norway. It is particularly well adapted to the cold, with long, thick, fur and a woolly undercoat and is perfectly happy bouncing through the snow in the depths of a Norwegian winter.[131] It is also one of the largest breeds of cats, weight up to 9kg (20 pounds). It is thought the ancestors of the cat were brought back from England by the Vikings around 1,000 years ago and could perhaps be the origin of the legendary *skogkatt*. The *skogkatt* is a mythical fairy cat who can climb impossibly steep rock faces. A pair of mythical cats (again, likely to be Norwegian forest cats) used to pull the chariot of the goddess Freya.

---

[131] I have seen a Norwegian forest cat doing just that. I was freezing even though I was in a thick skiing jacket – the cat was perfectly happy just in its fur.

The **Aphrodite** breed (above) was only officially recognised in 2017 and is the name given to pure breeding cats from Cyprus. As you know, the oldest evidence of cat domestication was found on the island, but these cats are believed to have a later (but still very old) origin. According to legend, Saint Helen of Constantinople sent two boat loads of cats to Cyprus from the Middle East in the fourth century AD in order to eradicate an infestation of snakes. The cats remain to this day as athletic hunters spanning the island from the coasts to the mountains.

The British shorthair is one of the oldest known breeds of cats, dating back to the first century AD when Roman invaders brought cats to Britain to keep their camps clear of snakes (there is a bit of a 'cats killing snakes' theme starting here). They are large, affectionate beasties who have been the inspiration of a number of famous cats. Their large, smiling face was used by Sir John Tenniel when he needed a model for the illustrations of the Cheshire Cat in *Alice's Adventures in Wonderland.* Although he speaks with an obvious Spanish accent, Puss in Boots in the *Shrek* films is also a British shorthair. In the real world the most famous British shorthair is probably the *I Can Has Cheezburger?* Internet meme star.

The Thai or **Wichien Maat** is a recently defined, but old cat breed from Thailand, related to, but distinct from, Siamese cats. Incredibly elegant cats, they have pale bodies and 'point colouration', that is to say dark ears, faces, tails and feet. This trait, also shared with Siamese cats, is actually temperature-sensitive albinism – the colder parts of their bodies become dark, the warmer parts remain light. Crazy as it may sound, if you put a pair of socks on one of these cats (the cat would obviously *hate* that) then over time the paws would lighten. This can be readily seen when, for instance, a cat has to be shaved for an operation. The fur on the now exposed (and cold) skin will initially grow back darker, before becoming light. Thais are very friendly, chatty cats (some humans who live with them might be inclined to say a bit *too* chatty). Their ancestor was the *wichienmaat* or 'moon diamond' which was first described in one of the earliest catalogues of cat breeds, the *Tamra Maeo* often referred to as 'Cat-Book Poems'. These beautiful manuscripts normally contain descriptions and illustrations of 17 breeds of cats and are believed to have been first drafted more than 300 years ago.

Louiethe27th

Turkish Van cats (above) have white bodies with colour on their tails at the top of their heads, and are believed to have originated from a race of pure white cats that lived around Lake Van in Turkey. They are excellent hunters and leapers – reputedly they can jump straight up onto the top of a refrigerator from the kitchen floor – but this is not what they are most famous for. Unlike most other breeds of domestic cat they do not hate water – indeed they seem to be fascinated by it, playing with water bowls and puddles and happily swimming when given the chance. Well, *maybe* they will happily swim – it appears the notion that all Turkish Van cats are keen and excellent swimmers may be a little bit fanciful. What is definitely true is that they can display dog-like behaviour and will play fetch with their humans, sometimes bringing over a toy to initiate the game.

Ankord

Finally **Maine Coons** (above), the largest of the domestic cat breeds. Like the Norwegian forest cat the Maine Coon is very well adapted to harsh winter conditions. Their thick fur is water resistant and particularly long on their rear so that they can, err, sit on the snow without their bum getting cold. They have particularly large paws which help prevent them sinking into the snow with long tufts of fur that keep their toes warm. Their tail is bushy and almost racoon-like, and as a result it does sink into the snow like a regular tail would; it also can be used as a cushion or scarf by the cat to keep out the worst of the elements. No one is really sure how they arose. One tale says that Queen Marie Antoinette attempted to flee France in 1793 to avoid execution and loaded her most precious possessions onto a ship. These included six of her favourite (possibly Siberian) cats. She, of course, met a grisly end, but the ship sailed to America with the cats and upon landing in Maine they bred with the local short-haired cats to create the beasts that we know today. This story is almost certainly untrue, but anyone who has seen a Maine Coon will agree that they have a distinctly regal bearing.

In the last 20 years there have been some astonishing developments in the breeding of cats, the most incredible of which has been the development of cloned cats. The first ever cloned cat (named CC, short for either 'CopyCat' or 'Carbon Copy') was born in December 2001. The cloning was carried out by scientists at Texas A&M University and a company called Genetic Savings & Clone Inc. – a short-lived commercial attempt to make a business out of cloning cats. Although CC was genetically identical to her genetic donor, a cat named Rainbow, she had different markings. This is because embryonic development plays a critical role in establishing the final markings of a cat. While the genes will be identical, there will always be variations in the embryonic development. CC lived to the ripe old age of 18, had four healthy kittens and seemed to show no ill effects of her unusual origin. Despite the fact that it is impossible to guarantee the creation of a physically identical duplicate of your favourite puss, a number of commercial cloning services exist today, charging $25,000–$35,000 per copy. It is totally understandable that someone would want to replace a much-loved pet, and the grief from their loss can be overwhelming, but a clone isn't the same as bringing that cat back to life. Sadly the original cat will have died, and should be mourned. The copy may be very similar physically and in temperament, but it won't be the same cat, it will have had a different upbringing and different experiences. Given how many lovely cats there are in shelters around the world desperate for a home it is hard to see how paying a fortune to clone your cat is nothing more than expensive, selfish self-indulgence.

Domestic Cat Senses

Cats experience the world very differently to humans. Obviously they are much smaller and run around on four legs and all that, but here I specifically mean through their senses. Cats have evolved to be incredibly efficient predators, and the senses that they possess today reflect that. Given that they are predators, does that mean that they have excellent eyesight? Well (because nothing is ever straightforward with cats) the answer is 'yes *and* no'. Cats are pretty nearsighted (in human terms) – an object that we could see clearly 200 metres away would need to be only 20 metres away for a cat to see it with the same degree of clarity. That may seem odd, but if you think about the kinds of things that cats hunt, there isn't much value in them being to see well over long distances – a mouse scampering across the grass a couple of hundred yards away is unlikely to end up being dinner for a hungry cat. What is much more important is that they can see clearly at short distances in poor light conditions. Cats need only around one seventh of the amount of light to see as effectively as humans do. In large part this is due to the *tapteum lucidum*, a reflective layer that sits behind the retina in the cat's eye. By bouncing the light back into the eye and essentially means that it can be used more than once. The tapteum is the reason that cats' eyes will often have, let's be honest, something of a demonic glow in photographs taken with a flash.

The reflective characteristics of cats' eyes led to a major improvement in road safety through the invention of, err, the 'cat's eye'. In 1934 Percy Shaw of Halifax, England was driving home late one foggy night along a road that had a steep drop off to one side. Unable to see the route clearly he was saved from disaster by the light of the car's headlights reflecting off the eyes of the cat that was sitting on the fence. This brush with death inspired him to invent reflective studs that could be set into roads enabling drivers to see the route even when there was no street lighting. Okay, so this one of the stories he told about how he came up with the idea; another was that he saw his headlights glinting off a tramline. I prefer the one about the cat. And let's face it, he didn't name his invention 'tramlines', did he?

Cats can see in colour, albeit with not as much richness as humans, but it is possible that they can see into the ultraviolet beyond our range of vision. It may seem as though cats sometimes have a second eyelid, under the main one. This is because they possess a *nictitating membrane* that closes in from the side when a cat closes its eye and serves to keep the eye protected and clean. We all know that it is hard to win a staring contest with a cat, and that is simply because they don't need to blink as often to keep their eyes lubricated with tears. This also certainly evolved to aid with predation – you don't want to be blinking the second a mouse pops out of its hole and miss it; every fraction of a second counts. Other than the fact that you will doubtless lose, initiating a staring contest with a cat is generally a bad idea. Cats can find the behaviour to be a threat or a challenge (think about how intently two rival cats will sit and stare at each other) so if you want to avoid stressing a cat out, don't attempt to hold eye contact with it.

Cats will sometimes stare intently at things that humans are unable to see, or at least unable to notice. They are not, as some suggest, seeing ghosts. Rather they are likely to be focusing on something – a tiny spider, a mote of dust – that either we are unable to discern or else simply would never occur to us to stare at. Also, it may seem as though they are staring intently, when in fact what they are doing is *listening* intently, which brings us nicely on to their hearing.

If your cat appears to react to a sound that you can't hear then chances are that is because they just did. Cats' hearing is both more sensitive than that of humans (but not incredibly so in lower ranges) and more broad. Cats can hear sounds at around 64khz, whereas humans can hear only up to around 20khz – they can hear higher pitches even than dogs. What they are also much better at than humans is pinpointing the origin of sounds. Their highly mobile ears enable them to locate the source of a sound coming from a metre away to within around 8 cm. That may not sound hugely impressive, but have you ever wandered around the kitchen wondering where that odd buzzing noise is coming from? A cat would be able to tell you in a second. If it could effectively communicate with you. And if it wanted to. Which it probably wouldn't. You may have heard tell that white cats with blue eyes are deaf? Well, they aren't. They have a slightly higher incidence of deafness than other cats but most of them can hear just fine. Similarly, 'odd-eyed cats' – that is cats with one blue eye and one eye of a different colour – are also said to be deaf, but they are only ever likely to be deaf on the side of their blue eye. If you live with one of these cats you know which side to call them from now.

It is fairly well known that dogs will respond to their names, but it might surprise you to learn that actually cats do as well. A research paper published in 2019 carried out an experiment with 78 cats where they were spoken to with four words that sounded like their names and one that actually was their name. The researchers found that there was a measurably different response from the cats when their actual name was spoken, even if it was being spoken by a total stranger.

Cats' sense of smell is simply amazing – something like 9-16 times better than ours. This is due to the fact that they have been 50-200 million odour receptors in their little twitchy noses, whereas we have a paltry five million.[132] This makes it incredibly difficult for us to comprehend how they perceive the world. A simple back garden will be a mass of olfactory information – scents they (and other cats) have left, the traces of smell prey animals have left behind, and the odours of us humans.

Cats are clearly fond of touch, but as with smell, it can create a world view that is alien to us. The 24 whiskers they have around their mouth and nose, along with the ones in their eyebrows and the couple they have on the back of their legs, feed signals into a part of the brain that is similar to the visual cortex. This enables them to build up a three-dimensional map of their environment – they can't 'see' through touch, but they can create an accurate rendering of what is about them. This has a very practical role to play when the cat is hunting. Due to the shape of their heads and the positioning of their eyes they can find it difficult to see things that are literally right under their nose (as small prey animals are likely to be). In these situations the whiskers around the cat's mouth will move forwards to create a basket shape which enables them to accurately detect the location of their prey.

---

[132] Even though we are comparatively bad at smelling things compared to other animals did you know that humans can detect *one trillion* different odours? Scientists used to think it was just 10,000 but hey, science is the process of building up an ever more accurate understanding of the universe through study and experimentation.

I have already mentioned that cats lack the taste receptors to detect sweet things – a fact that was only discovered in 2005. This is the result of a genetic mutation that occurred very early in the evolutionary history of cats, and it is found in all living species of cat today. It is believed that this is why cats today are obligate carnivores – that is they can survive by only eating prey animals, as their digestive systems are not adapted to cope with plant material. Dogs, on the other hand, are facultative, or scavenging, carnivores. Meat is what they primarily eat, but they can munch on plants alone if they really have to. Plants usually taste good to eat because the carbohydrates in them make them sweet. For millions of years cats have been unable to taste this sweetness and have gone for meat instead, and their guts have adapted as a response. There is an increasing trend among well-meaning cat owners to give their cat a vegetarian, or even vegan, diet, to prevent animals being killed to feed their pet. This, for the reasons described above, is a really bad idea. Cats rely upon the meat that they eat for certain proteins, such as taurine – they are unable to synthesize it themselves. While you can buy vegetarian cat food that is supplemented with taurine and other additives, the vast majority of vets believe that in order for your cat to thrive you have to feed it meat.

Domestic Cat Behaviour

If you have spent much time with cats[133] you will know that they have a range of distinctive behaviours. Doubtless there will have been times when you have thought 'huh, I wonder why they do that?'. Well, this section will hopefully answer all of those questions, and more! Okay, more honestly it will *try* to answer those questions – it turns out that a lot of the time we really *aren't that certain*[134] exactly why cats do the things that they do, but various scientists have taken some educated guesses over the years.

Why do cats purr?

Before we talk about why cats purr, let's first look at *how* cats purr. The answer is, um, no one knows for sure. Now this came as something of a surprise to me; I thought that it would be pretty well established that the purring noise was made by... well, you know, a *thing* vibrating inside of the cat. One theory is that the gap between the cat's vocal cords – called the *glottis* – is made to expand and contract rapidly, creating the purring sound as the cat breathes in and out.

Not all species of cat can purr. In fact, no species of cat has the ability to both purr *and* roar. Lions, tigers, panthers and leopards are all members of a genera called the *roaring cats* because, wait for it, they can roar. However, because the natural world can't always be categorised into straightforward boxes, there is an exception. The snow leopard can purr, but it can't roar, even though it is a member of the group of roaring cats. Some scientists believe that it should therefore be put into a new genus of its own. As far as we can tell the snow leopards themselves really don't care.[135]

Purring in cats is thought to have developed as a means by which the kitten and its mother can mutually communicate reassurance. If the mother is purring, the kitten knows that everything is okay in the world; if the kitten is purring then the mother knows that it

---

[133] And why wouldn't you have done, eh?

[134] Just for fun (depending upon your definition of the word 'fun') I am going to keep track in this section of the number of times I say words to the effect of 'we just don't know for sure'.

[135] I have no basis for this statement. I simply thought that it would be an 'amusing' thing to say.

is doing just fine. In more grown-up cats, purring is (you have probably already worked this out) a sign of contentment and being relaxed, which is why the chilled-out cat you are stroking on your lap starts purring. It can also be a way of signalling to others that the purring cat is not a threat.

What you may not have known is that cats have two types of purr. One is the regular 'I am happy' purr that scientists term the 'non-solicitation purr'. The cat doesn't want anything, all is good. Then there is the second type of purr, which has a higher frequency. This seems to be a way for the cat to signal to humans that it wants something – that 'something' usually being food. This type of purr is called the 'solicitation purr'. If a cat starts purring as it trots along by your heels as you walk into the kitchen then you are likely to be hearing the solicitation purr.

An experiment was once carried out whereby 50 people were played the solicitation and non-solicitation purrs of 10 different cats (without being told which was which). The lower non-solicitation purrs were judged to be more pleasant and relaxing. The solicitation purrs, in contrast, were found to be more urgent and less pleasant.[136] It has been suggested that solicitation purrs have developed to be at a higher frequency because humans are hard-wired to find it hard to ignore high-frequency pleas, as a result of raising our own crying infants.[137]

Cat's don't only purr if they are happy (or because they want something). They will also purr if they are in pain. When a female cat is giving birth she will often purr, despite the agony. It is thought that this is a form of self-relaxation and may also trigger the release of painkilling hormones. This would also explain why injured cats will often purr. It is also thought that purring helps the healing of muscles and bones, and can even help the maintenance of muscle tone and bone density. Because cats spend so much time asleep (or at least not moving very much), there is a risk that their muscles and bones would start to weaken. It seems that the low-frequency

---

[136] Yes, I have attempted to tell the difference between the two types of purr of the cats that I live with. No, I haven't been able to notice a difference.

[137] Some new parents suggest that after a couple of months it is possible to ignore the high-frequency pleas of babies. At least a little bit. I think this theory still holds, though.

hum of a purr is an efficient way of keeping them stimulated. This is why a cat who has been kept in a cage to restrict its movement after an injury or operation will still remain pretty lithe and strong. This property of purring has led to an application that is literally out of this world. Astronauts on the International Space Station find that, in the absence of gravity, their bone density declines incredibly quickly. A recent trial that applied low-frequency vibrations to their legs during a five-month mission turned out to be an excellent way of maintaining their strength.[138]

Why do cats miaow?
The simple answer to this question is that they are trying to tell you something. But here is the really interesting thing: they are specifically trying to tell a *human being* something.[139] Adult cats do *not* miaow at each other. They will growl, hiss, yowl and purr at each other, for sure – but they won't miaow. Kittens will miaow as a means of communicating to their mothers that they are lost, or they are cold, scared or hungry, and it seems that cats have learned to continue this behaviour as a means of communicating with humans.

Augustus Binu

---

[138] This is totally true. Google it if you don't believe me.
[139] Pretty wild, huh?

Humans are, truth be told, pretty useless communicators as far as cats are concerned. Unlike other cats we are *terrible* at understanding their body language. We may be able to work out that a cat that is thrashing its tail is annoyed, but we miss the complex array of messages cats convey from the positioning of their ears, the movement of their body, their posture, and so on. Next time you see two cats meeting each other for the first time, watch their bodies and movements with care as they convey fear or friendliness, submission or dominance, interest or hatred (and, of course, be ready to step in quickly in case they start fighting).

Cats have, therefore, worked out that in order to communicate with the lumbering, two-legged giants that they share their world with, they have got get vocal. A miaow can be:

- A simple greeting: 'Hello!'
- A demand for food: 'I'm hungry'
- A demand for attention: 'Fuss me!'
- A demand for a toy: 'My mouse has rolled under the sofa!'
- A demand for a door to be opened: 'Let me in! Let me out!'

If you live with a cat then you have probably worked out which miaow means which. Though of course they can mean multiple things at the same time: 'Let me in, give me some food, and then give me a fuss!'.[140]

Why do cats bring humans dead animals?

If you have lived with an outdoor cat you may have been surprised to find a small, dead animal such as a bird or a mouse left on your doormat. You may have been equally (but probably less happily) surprised to find a similar corpse deposited somewhere in your house. If you are even more 'lucky'[141] you may have found that your cat has brought a live animal into the house which you then have to pursue, catch, and hopefully release back into the wild.

In such situations you may well have thought 'why has the cat done this?' (or perhaps, more realistically, 'why the HELL has the

---

[140] How many human languages offer such efficiency of communication?
[141] Actually unlucky.

cat done this?'). The most popular reason you will hear given is that the cat has brought you a 'present' to show you how much it loves you. While we don't know for sure,[142] the reality is probably a little bit different. One theory is that the cat is simply being generous – sharing its kills with you in the same way that you share food with it (okay, so you don't eat cat food, but the cat doesn't know that). It's another way of saying 'hey, we're in the same group and we support each other'. Alternatively it could be a way of asking for more attention – 'hey look at the nice mouse I bought you, now, will you stroke me a bit more to say thank you?'.

Neither of these theories explains why a cat would bring you a live animal though. A possible explanation for that behaviour is that the cat is trying to *teach* you. Mother cats will bring their kittens both dead and live prey to teach them how to hunt. Dead prey for them to bat around a bit and discover that these things are good to eat; live (but often injured) prey for them to actually hunt down and kill for themselves. Neutered female cats in particular bring prey back to their humans, and the theory is that these cats, having either not had kittens at all, or not being able to in future, consider their humans to be their kittens. It is pretty clear to these cats that humans are *terrible* hunters because, duh, they never, ever seem to catch anything. It is the job of the cat then to try and teach them how to do it. It must be terribly frustrating for the poor beast that no matter how many animals – dead or alive – they bring to their humans, the stupid apes never seem to work out how to actually hunt anything.

Now this hasn't been recommended by 'proper' scientists[143] but the next time your cat brings you an animal why not try getting down on all fours and batting it around a bit to demonstrate that you are learning? It sounds crazy, but it might just work. Okay, so it probably *won't* work but it would be kinda funny if you gave it a try. You never know, you might just end up helping science in the process. And, who knows, perhaps improving your hunting skills.

---

[142] That makes twice I've had to play the 'don't know' card so far.

[143] To be clear, it hasn't been suggested by *improper* scientists either.

Why do cats 'chatter' at birds?

You may have seen a cat start making excited 'chattering' noises when it spots a bird out of the window (or even on TV or a computer screen). It is pretty clear that the cat is really very excited, but why does it chatter? There are couple of possible explanations. One is simply that it is just excited; adrenaline surges through it and it can't help but chatter in response. Another (I am, I have to say, less convinced by this one) that the cat is practising its 'death bite'. Both of these answers are perhaps a little strange if you think of the cat not as inside, looking at a bird, but outside, trying to hunt it. Making any kind of noise as it stalks a piece of prey is going to be a pretty bad idea for a cat – the sound is likely to act as a warning. The experience of the author bears this out – when I have seen cats stalking outside they have been as close to totally silent as they can manage.

There is another theory, but to be honest I think that this is reaching a bit.[144] Margays are small wildcats that live in the jungles of Central and South America (for more on them see the Cats in the Wild chapter). They are almost unbelievably gorgeous creatures – as you will see later. In 2005 researchers found that one of these cats made calls that mimicked the cry of baby tamarin monkeys. A group of tamarins, intrigued and confused by the calls, went to investigate – only to be surprised by the margay (in this case all of the monkeys escaped unhurt). This incident supported reports of margays and other cats such as pumas and jaguars copying the calls of their prey in order to attract them. Could it be that when a domestic cat is chattering it is trying to sound like a bird? I'm not convinced, but you may think otherwise!

Why do cats turn round and round in circles before settling down?

You will almost certainly have seen a cat on your lap, or on a bed, or in some other cat-friendly spot, turn round and round multiple times before finally getting comfortable and start snoozing.[145] There are numerous theories as to *exactly* why cats do this, and you will be doubtless amazed to hear that *we don't know for sure*. The one

---

[144] Actually, a lot.

[145] You have even said to a cat doing this on you lap words to the effect of 'Oh, come on, just settle down!'. I know that I have.

that I was always told was that cats in the wild did this to flatten down grass to make a more comfortable nest for themselves. Alternatively it was a way of inspecting the ground to make sure it was free of insects or poisonous animals and other nasty critters that could harm or disturb the slumbering beastie. It could even be that it allowed the cat to assess the wind direction, and so ensure that it could smell the approach of a potential predator. One amazing fact[146] is that cats north of the equator always turn anti-clockwise before to sleep, while their brethren south of the equator always turn clockwise! Check this out next time you see a cat sleepily turning around.

Why do cats 'knead' humans they are sitting on?

If you have sat with a contented cat on your lap then often it will start to 'knead' you with its paws. Sometimes gently. Sometimes vigorously. And if it has sharp claws sometimes *painfully.* This is generally a sign that the cat is happy and relaxed. It is thought that this behaviour is the cat harking back to when it was a kitten, and it would rhythmically push its paws into its mother's belly in order to stimulate her milk production so that it could get a good feed. So if it is happening to you, then it is probably that the cat is thinking of you as a massive, human-shaped mother which I think we can all agree is pretty sweet.

This kneading behaviour (which doesn't always happen when a cat is sitting on a human – they can do it to other cats, dressing gowns, soft toys and so on) is also thought to be simply a way for the cat to de-stress, relax, and generally feel safe and secure. So even though it might hurt from time to time do remember that it means that your cat is in a good place. And also perhaps to wear a thicker pair of jeans next time.

Why do cats wash so much?

The simple answer to this question is to keep their fur clean and tidy. Cats have a lot of fur, and left unattended it will become matted with dirt and full of debris. Washing is also a way for cats

---

[146] This isn't a 'fact'. I just made it up. What are the odds that it ends up getting cited by blog or in a Wikipedia entry by someone who didn't bother reading this footnote?

to remove fleas and other parasites from their bodies. A cat's tongue is covered with little barbs (if you have every been licked by a cat you will know that it feels a bit like being rubbed with a piece of soft, wet sandpaper) and these barbs are perfectly designed to groom and clean the fur. Washing also helps to spread oils that are produced in glands at the bottom of each hair across the coat, keeping it rich and glossy.

A cat is not keeping clean simply for the sake of being clean. Were it to not remove traces of food and dirt it would develop a more distinct scent, making it easier for a predator to track it.

Finally, it also appears to be the case that cats wash themselves simply because it feels good (which also helps to explain why they like it if humans stroke or brush them). Given that they spend around 50% of their (not very many – see below) waking hours washing, I think that is probably for the best.

Why do cats sleep so much?

Cats sleep a lot. Seriously. A lot. This probably isn't news to you, but did you know that cats on average sleep between 16 and 20 hours a day? Young kittens will generally sleep 24 hours a day, with their snoozing time reducing as they age, but increasing again as they become elderly cats. The reason that they spend so much time in the land of nod is because of their evolutionary past. Before humans took on the role of food providers to felines, cats would have acquired all of their food through hunting. Hunting is a pretty draining activity for a cat, demanding large amounts of energy and leaving it exhausted. That may seem obvious if you are thinking about lions on the savannah, furiously chasing after antelope, but it is also true for their smaller cousins who share our homes.

It is, for sure, a lot easier to kill a mouse than an antelope, and based upon the number of dead 'offerings' cats bring to humans it may seem that catching dinner is very little trouble at all for a cat. What you aren't seeing is the hours spent prowling around trying to find the mice, the time spent focused with great intensity waiting for one to appear, and all of the dramatic chases where the mouse manages to get away.

Domestic cats sleep so much as a way of recharging themselves after a hunt, and conserving energy for the next one. It doesn't matter that for many their 'hunts' will involve little more than mewing pitifully every time you open the fridge, their sleeping patterns developed over the course of millions of years before generous humans came along. You may have noticed that the weather affects the sleeping pattern of your cat. If it is cold and wet then the cat is likely to sleep more because these are poor conditions for hunting. Similarly cats tend to sleep less when the weather is clear and warm.

Many people think that cats are nocturnal – that their natural inclination is to sleep during the day and become active at night. Given how much cats sleep during the day this is a pretty understandable conclusion. In reality cats are *crepuscular*, which is to say that they are most active at dawn and at dusk – the best times for them to be hunting – and that they tend to spend most of the time in between sleeping. If you have ever wondered why your cat gets the 'zoomies' and starts rushing around in the evening (often just after it has been fed) or why it will wake you up at 5am demanding food or attention (or, most likely, both) then that is why – these are natural times for them to be most active.

Do cats dream?
Having established that cats spent the majority of their lives asleep, it is pretty reasonable to wonder if they are dreaming as they are doing so. The answer is, probably, 'yes'. The French sleep scientist Michel Jouvet (among many other things he identified REM sleep in humans) turned his attention to cats in the late 1950s and early 60s. Jouvet found that cats experience REM sleep much as humans do. What do they dream of? Well, much like humans we believe that they dream of day-to-day things, which for a cat will be hunting, exploring, eating, and generally being cute. Have you ever seeing a cat twitching its paws, as if running, while it is asleep? Or chattering much as it would at a bird if it were awake? You may have thought that the cat is dreaming of hunting when this happens; if so, you would be correct (as far as we can tell). Normally both cats and humans experience something call muscle atonia when they are sleeping – a form of paralysis that prevents them from physically

acting out their dream. Sometimes this paralysis is not perfect, which explains why you will see little twitching paws as a cat sleeps.

Why do cats sometimes try to wash humans?

Because we are filthy, dirty creatures. Okay, so that isn't the reason (or at least it hopefully isn't true of the readers of this book!). Most of the time it is simply a sign of affection. Cats will often wash their litter-mates, or other unrelated cats if they are living happily with them. It is a way of reinforcing social bonds and demonstrating that they are all part of the same group. Sometimes it could be that you have a tasty scent on your skin from cooking (if you have just chopped up some fresh fish and a cat starts licking your hands, odds are that is the reason rather than just simple love). Alternatively it could be a scent in a lotion or shampoo or perfume that is attractive to the cat – or even that the cat dislikes it and wants to try and get rid of it.

Finally, it could also be a way for the cat to show that it is, err, the boss of you. While most feral cats are solitary, some, where there are plentiful supplies of food, such as on farms, live together in colonies. Cats in these colonies will often perform what is call *allogrooming* – that is, social grooming between members of this group. Studies have found that the more dominant (and potentially aggressive) cats tend to do the majority of the grooming, with the subordinate cats being the ones receiving the attention. This grooming behaviour reduces tension within the group and helps maintain dominance hierarchies.

Fun fact![147] Rabbits have the opposite grooming/dominance approach. That is to say that the dominant rabbit(s) in a group will be groomed by their subordinates – often pushing their heads forward to demand a washing session. The upshot of this is that if you live with both a cat *and* a rabbit then the cat is likely to end up washing the rabbit; however, both of them will think that they are the one in charge!

---

[147] Fun to me, anyhow.

Why do cats like to climb into boxes (and other small spaces)?

Even if you have never lived with cats you will probably know (thanks to the plethora of online videos showing this behaviour) that cats really love to squeeze themselves into small spaces – particularly cardboard boxes. And then sit there, generally looking really cute. It may come as a surprise for you to learn that ancient cats, living in the wild, never encountered cardboard boxes, So how has this behaviour arisen?

Well, no one is *really* sure[148] (can you detect a theme here when it comes to human understanding of cat behaviour?). The best guess is that in the wild cats like to find small spaces that they can cram themselves into in order to hide, and living in modern homes, cardboard boxes (and other similar items) provide good options to do so. Why do cats in the wild want to hide? Two reasons. The first is that they want to feel safe and secure from predators. They don't want to sleep, or relax, somewhere out in the open where they might be attacked. They want to curl up in a space where they are very unlikely to be found. The second is that they are hiding because *they* are the predator. If they are all tucked away, hidden from view, then it is much more likely that an unsuspecting bird or mouse will wander within attacking distance and the cat can then pounce.

Why do cats like to chase laser pointers?

Even if you haven't tried this specifically, you might have noticed your cat being transfixed by a moving reflection of the sun on a wall, from your wristwatch for example. It all comes down to the cat's hunting instincts and the nature of its eyesight. Cats have evolved to be super-sensitive to movement, and their retinas are particularly good at picking this up in the low light levels of twilight, when cats are most active (see above).

There are two types of cell in the retina: humans have more of the 'cones', great for picking out different colours and fine details, whereas cats have more 'rods', which identify movement and objects in low-contrast settings. So while we're standing there admiring the pretty leaves on a tree, the cat has already zipped off and caught the shrew scampering underneath it.

---

[148] I make that four.

Hence the fact that your cat will happily 'play' with the dot from a laser pointer if you have one – although some cats will eventually get antsy at the lack of possible follow-through from this inconclusive hunt.

Why are cats afraid of cucumbers?

At some point over the last couple of years you will probably have seen a video where a human stealthily puts a cucumber on the floor behind a cat. When the cat notices it they go, as we say in Britain, absolutely bonkers – sometimes leaping several feet straight up into the air. What is it about these long green salad items that freaks them out so much? First off, cats are hyper-aware of their surroundings. Something large appearing close to them without them noticing is always going to startle them somewhat. This alone does not however explain the intensity of the reaction to cucumbers. The best guess[149] is a pretty simple one (which you may well have come up with) – cucumbers look a bit like snakes. They too are long and thin, and also are able to move incredibly silently and hence sneak up on a cat without being noticed, just like your stealthy cucumber insertion. Cats are genetically hard wired to be very wary of snakes. It doesn't matter if they have lived in a house their entire lives and never seen one, nor indeed that they live in a country such as Ireland where snakes have never lived (spoiler: they weren't banished from the country by St Patrick as the myth goes – they were never there in the first place).

The most important thing to remember is that whatever the explanation, surprising a cat with a cucumber will *really stress it out* so please don't do it, no matter how good a video you think it might make.

Why do cats like to play with string?

Think of a cat at play and you will often think of it batting furiously at a piece of string being waved by a person, dragged across the floor for them or simply just being *there*. Why do they do this? Well, as with a lot of cat behaviour no one really knows for certain,[150] but it

---

[149] In other words 'We don't really know'. Five.

[150] And there is six.

is most likely that the string elicits a hunting response in the cat. Why would a long, thin thing do that? Well as we have learned from the cucumbers, cats are very familiar with snakes, and in the past if one had got close to them they would certainly have tried to kill it or scare it off. String is also very similar to the tails of mice and rats, frequent prey for cats. Cats don't just catch string though; once they have subdued it you will often see then scoop it up into their mouths and give it a jolly good chew. The explanation for that is a little bit more gruesome – string, particularly red string, is thought to resemble the blood-covered intestines of recently killed prey and so kitty has a chomp on it in case it is a meal.

Why do cats headbutt people?
So, there you are, lying in bed, and your cat jumps up and starts headbutting you in the face. Cute as hell, right, but why does the cat do it? Sometimes it will be simply a sign of affection or a means of gaining attention. But not all of the time. When a cat headbutts you it is not just simply mushing a lovely ball of fluff into you; it is marking you with its scent. Cats have a load of scent glands on their heads (as well as on their paws, the base of their tails, and, err, an anal scent glad). By marking you with its scent, a cat it can be simply marking its territory (but given that humans have an irritating tendency to move, it isn't hugely effective at that). More often though it is marking you as being part of their colony space. It is, for want of a better term, indicating that you are a 'safe' thing to be around. Not quite as cute as being way of expressing its love for you, but *pretty* cute nonetheless.

Why do cats sit on laptops?[151]
Because I never get tired of typing the words 'no one really knows for sure', can I just start by saying 'no one really knows for sure'?[152] Good. Thank you. The most obvious and likely explanation is that cats like attention, and their stupid human is sitting there paying attention to something else that *isn't them* so the best way to make sure that this odd thing stops receiving attention and that they start

---

[151] (and books, and magazines, and anything else you might want to be using)
[152] A clear seven.

getting it is to simply *sit on it*. There is also the added bonus that, in the case of laptops, they are usually toasty warm. Win-win.

Some people have suggested that cats also like to mimic the behaviours of their favourite humans. If you are showing this thing so much attention, then heck! they will too. It has even been suggested that putting a large, open book (or, if you have one, another laptop) next to the thing that you are using will attract a cat who wants to copy you. I have to say that given that the 'evidence' supporting this theory appears to be couple of pictures on Twitter I am not wholly convinced.

Why do cats push things off surfaces and watch them fall onto the floor? (sometimes over and over and over again)

Because it is fun. Well, maybe that is the reason. The honest answer is (surprise, surprise!) no one really sure.[153] It has been suggested that patting a thing around on a table, only for it to fall off onto the floor, is a *bit* like chasing a mouse that manages to escape at the last second. But let's be honest here, that's just a guess and frankly I am sure that you could come up with a different one that is just as convincing. It certainly seems to be the case that sometimes cats will push things onto the floor as a way of getting attention from their humans. But they also push things onto the floor when no one is around. Whatever the reason, I am pretty certain that they get something out of the process, otherwise they wouldn't keep doing it!

Do cats like being stroked?

If you have ever lived with cats then the answer to this question must seem pretty obvious – most of the time, most cats like to be stroked. It came as a surprise to many then when a scientific study published in 2013 was reported to have discovered that cats *don't* like being stroked and that in fact it stressed them out. As is (alas) often the way with science reporting, the actual findings were very different to the headlines that appeared in the press (a major UK national newspaper ran with *'Want to show your cat affection? Think twice before stroking it: Our feline friends can become stressed when touched'*.)

---

[153] And there we have eight!

What the research paper actually found is that cats who are already stressed because of the environment in which they are living (because they are living with other cats, or haven't properly socialised with humans) will sometimes allow themselves to be stroked, even though they don't enjoy it, and this stresses them out.

We think that the most important lesson here is to be distrustful of newspaper headlines that report counter-intuitive scientific 'discoveries' and always try to read the original research, if you can.

Why do cats eat grass?
We generally think of cats as being simple carnivores – they live on a diet of meat. In fact, to be technical about it, they are *obligate carnivores*, which is to say that they only need meat to live. (You may be wondering, how do they get things like vitamin C then, which humans get from eating fruit and vegetables? The answer is that they synthesise it in their bodies from glucose. Among mammals only primates – of which we are of course one species – guinea pigs, and fruit bats are unable to do the same. Isn't nature fascinating?) It isn't that uncommon though to see them munching on blades of grass, or other plants. Most people tend to think that this is a sign that the cat is ill, and that it is eating the grass to make itself sick. This is not an unreasonable assumption, because often after you see at cat eat grass it will throw up (or, if you have the misfortune to find cat vomit somewhere around your home, it will sometimes have chewed-up grass in it).

As with many things cat related, the answer is a little more complicated than that. Because cats lack the enzymes to digest grass, it can cause them to throw up, and one possible reason that they eat the stuff is because they are feeling a bit poorly – they feel that they have eaten something that isn't agreeing with them and they want to get it out of their system as quickly as possible. Grass is also thought to act as a laxative, and so it can work at, well, getting things out of the other end as well if the problem has progressed too far to be thrown up.

This explanation makes a great deal of sense; however, it doesn't seem to the whole story. A large-scale study of 1,000 cat owners[154]

<hr>

[154] (I should say at this point that I don't really like the term 'cat owner' – I don't think

who observed their cats for three hours a day over a number of weeks reported that only around 25% of cats threw up after eating grass. It has been suggested that this is an ancient behaviour that helps them remove intestinal parasites, and hairballs, from their systems. Grass is a good source of fibre, and this helps with, well, getting everything out. This could be the reason that cats like to chew up paper and cardboard so much – in the absence of grass it is a decent substitute.[155]

Grass also happens to be rich in vitamin B and so cats could also be eating it simply as a dietary supplement. They can't pop to the health food store and grab vitamin pills the way people do, so this is the next best thing for them. The real answer is that probably all of these things are true (and likely some more besides we haven't thought of yet). One thing is clear, cats do seem to need, and indeed like, to eat grass. This is why if you live with a cat that doesn't have access to a patch of lawn outside you will sometimes find it chewing on plants. If that is the case for you, please take care! Ornamental house plants can contain toxins that are fatal to cats. As an alternative buy (or plant yourself) a simple pot of grass and keep it somewhere that the cat can easily access.

Why does catnip make cats go crazy?

First off, it makes sense to talk about what catnip actually is. Catnip, or to give it its scientific name, *Nepeta cataria* is a perennial herbaceous plant related to mint, which grows up to one metre (three feet) tall. It contains a compound called *nepetalactone* which, when inhaled by a cat will make it go, well, a little bit crazy – licking at the plant, purring, and generally being pretty ecstatic. It will probably come as no surprise to you that we *don't really know* why it has this effect on cats. It is thoughts that it is perhaps similar to cat pheromones, which is why they react to it so vigorously. Catnip reacts tend to last for between five and 15 minutes, after which time the cat's olfactory receptors become saturated by the chemical and the reaction subsides.

---

that anyone ever really *owns a cat*. I prefer to think of myself as a human who happens to live with cats, but I am digressing.)

[155] Let's be honest. That's a long-winded way of saying 'We don't know for sure'. That makes nine, thank you and goodnight.

Not all cats react to catnip (as you may well have found yourself) – something like 65-80% of them respond to it, not always positively. It is thought that there is a genetic cause of catnip sensitivity, and some cats simply don't possess the gene that makes them susceptible to it. Catnip is not the only plant to cause such reactions; silver vine and valerian root have similar effects. Nor is it only domestic moggies who go crazy for it. Leopards, cougars, lions and tiger have all been seen to exhibit catnip responses. You may be wondering, 'Hmmm, if it does this to cats, what would it do to a person? Should I have a little nibble to find out?' Amazingly, that is not such a bad idea. Catnips has been used as a sedative and relaxant in traditional medicine for centuries. Sometimes it is brewed into tea, or used as a poultice, or even smoked. Your cat, however, may not be too impressed if you steal its stash of catnip to make a quick brew.

Amazing Cats

All cats are, of course, amazing, but some are, shall we say, just a little more amazing than others. This could be because of their physical characteristics, their behaviour, or even their owners. Let's have a look at some of the most notable ones.

Superlative cats

There is no one answer to the question 'What is the *largest* domestic cat ever to have lived?' for the simple reason that you can define 'large' in a number of different ways. The *longest* known domestic cat was a Maine Coon named Stewie, who was 123 cm (four feet) from the tip of his nose to the tip of his tail. An 'average' shorthair cat (not that any cat is truly average) is closer to 70 cm long. He was a certified therapy animal who would be taken to meet senior citizens so that they could give him a fuss. Another Maine Coon, Cygnus Regulus Powers, has the longest ever recorded tail for a domestic cat, an impressive 45 cm (18 inches) long. His tail is so long that he accidentally trails it in things without realising it. A regular cat's tail is more like 30 cm (one foot) long. The record for the tallest cat is 48 cm (19 inches), roughly twice that of a regular domestic cat. This record, however, is held by a savannah cat, which is a cross between a domestic cat and a serval wild cat, so that doesn't really feel like it ought to count. One 'record' which thankfully is not awarded any more is for the *heaviest* cat, for the obvious reason that with cats, as with humans, being chronically overweight is damaging to health.

The cat with the *most toes* in the world is a beastie from Minnesota called, appropriately, Paws. Paws has a total of 28 toes, an extra three on each front paw and an additional one on each back paw.[156] Paws is a *polydactyl cat*: she possesses a genetic trait caused by a mutation that controls the regulation of the sonic hedgehog (SHH) gene in the limbs. Yes, there is a gene named after Sonic the Hedgehog. As I mentioned earlier, cats with extra toes were considered to be lucky by sailors and that is possibly why significant populations of them are now found in New England. The writer Ernest Hemingway was a fan of polydactyl cats, having been given a six-toed beastie by a ship's captain. Many shared his home in Key West, Florida and today, nearly 60 years after his death, more than 25 polydactyl cats live there still.

It is hard to say which cat is the *furriest* but the cat that holds the world record for the *longest fur* is a Himalayan-Persian cross-breed named 'Colonel Meow' that has 23 cm (9 inch) long fur. Do have a look for a picture of him online – he is a quite ridiculously furry cat, but luckily his humans take care of him by brushing him thoroughly three times a week.

If you have ever lived with cats, it probably won't come as much of a surprise to you to learn that they have *a lot* of hair. A cat has around 10,000 hairs per square centimetre on its back, and around 20,000 for the same area on its belly. To put this in context, the average human has around 100,000 hairs on their head, the equivalent number to 5 square centimetres (or less than one square inch) of a cat's belly. How many hairs does the average cat have in total? Well, we can work it out if we know the average skin area for a cat. Luckily for us (but very unluckily for the cats involved) a 1967 study came up with a formula for working out the skin area of a cat based upon its weight. The surface area in square centimetres is 388.4 x (weight of cat in kilograms) + 896.5. So for a cat that weighs 4 kg the surface area would be 2,450 square centimetres. With an average of 15,000 hairs per square centimetre that gives a total of around 37 million hairs.

The total surface area of all of that hair is about the same as a ping-pong table, which helps to explain why cats spend up to 40% of their time washing – there is an awful lot of hair to keep clean. That may sound like a lot, but there are even hairier beasties out there. A beaver typically has 300 million hairs, and a sea otter, with

---

[156] Her paws look very cute. Google 'cat most toes' to find pictures of her.

around 165,000 hairs per square centimetre (1 million hairs per square inch) can have 800 million hairs in total. Cats shed their hair year round (as you will have probably realised) but go through two major sheds each year. Once in the spring to lose their thick winter coat, and again in the autumn to make room for new winter fur. These sheddings are based upon the seasons, specifically day length not temperature, so indoor cats will experience them just the same as outdoor cats.

Domestic cats will generally live up to around 15-20 years (assuming that they avoid injury or disease) but there are a number of cats who have lived far longer. The *oldest* known cat, Creme Puff, lived to be 38 years and three days old, and more than a dozen are known to have lived 30 years or more. You will have probably heard tell of 'cat years' as a means of working out the age of a cat in human terms – it is typically said that one cat year is equivalent to seven human years (which would mean that Creme Puff lived to be more than 250 years old). As with many things in life, it is not actually that simple. A more accurate measure used by vets (which applies to cats who are two or more years old) is to say that to work out the human age of a cat, multiply its age by four and add sixteen. So a five-year-old cat would be akin to a 36-year-old human, and one who was 15 would be the equivalent of around 76. This feels about right to us, but it would mean still that Creme Puff lived to be about 150 years old.

It is difficult to say which is the *fastest* domestic cat – getting a cat to run at full speed, along a measured route, at a time when there is a human around is pretty much impossible. There is broad consensus however that if we were ever able to find out which the fastest cat is, it would be a member of the Egyptian Mau breed. Maus have particularly long back legs and a special flap of skin that runs from the back of their knee to their side which enables their legs to stretch back further than regular domestic cats, increasing the length of their stride and hence their speed. They have been recorded at running more than 48 kph (30 mph). To put that in some context, Usain Bolt on his record-breaking 100 metre run achieved a speed a little under 45 kph. Even your standard, non-pedigree moggie is likely to be able to match his pace, albeit for fairly short distances at a time. If you consider the speed a cat can achieve relative to its body length, it is even more impressive. The average cat has a body length that is around one quarter that of the average human, so you could say that the relative speed it reaches is closer to 100 mph (160 kph). Mice can only run at about 8 mph (around 13 kph) which explains why our feline friends are so good at hunting them down.

Another amazing characteristic of cats is their ability to survive huge falls. The furthest a cat has been confirmed to have fallen and survived is 32 stories (more than 100 metres or over 300 feet) – the cat in question received only minor injuries and was 'good to go' in two days. There have been other cases of cats falling more than 25 storeys (80 metres, 250 feet) and walking away without any injury. It would be wrong to think that cats are essentially indestructible when it comes to falling, though. A study of 132 cats known to have fallen from great heights found that 90% of them survived; however, two-thirds of them required the attentions of a vet afterwards, and roughly half of those were likely to have died had they not been treated. Nonetheless, that is a pretty incredible set of results. Had 132 humans fallen the same distances *all* of them would have required hospital treatment and many more (indeed probably most of them) would have died from their injuries.

There are a couple of reasons why cats have this uncanny survival ability. The first is that they have a relatively low terminal velocity (that is the maximum speed they will reach when falling). The terminal velocity of a cat is around 95 kph (60 mph) and they would reach this speed falling from a height of around 40 metres (130 feet). That means that the cat who fell 32 storeys would have been travelling no faster when they hit the ground than if they had jumped out of a plane at 10,000 feet. A human being on the other hand will reach around 200 kph (120 mph). It has been suggested that cats that fall from sufficient height to reach their terminal velocity may actually suffer from fewer injuries than cats that fall from lower heights – and there is some evidence to suggest that this is true (though the study has been questioned on the basis that cats who didn't survive such falls would never get taken to a vet and their details recorded). The reason behind this is that once a cat reaches its terminal velocity it relaxes as it falls, spreading out its paws and so making a shape a little like a flying squirrel (or a human in a wingsuit). By creating a larger profile in this way, their air resistance is increased, and their speed is reduced by 20-25%. Another factor that makes the survivability of falling cats even more impressive is that the ones known to have fallen from great heights have, in the main, fallen (unsurprisingly) from tall buildings, which means that they have landed on concrete or tarmac. Were they to have landed on a soft meadow then even more of them would have been able to walk away unharmed.

You have heard it said that a falling cat will more or less always land on its feet, and this is, surprisingly, pretty much true. Cats have a 'righting reflex' – as they fall they turn their bodies around to ensure that their feet are facing downwards. This is such an interesting (and unusual) trait that it has been studied in considerable detail. There are three stages to the process:

- The cat bends its body in the middle (helped by a lack of collarbone and very flexible spine) – this enables the front and back half of its body to rotate in opposite directions.
- Then it tucks in its front legs and extends its back legs, causing the front half of its body to rotate by as much as 90 degrees, while the back half rotates hardly at all.
- Finally it tucks in its back legs and extends its front legs, causing its back half to rotate to a similar extent.[157]

Landing legs down is hugely important for the survival of the cat, as its legs are *excellent* shock absorbers and significantly cushion the impact. You may be wondering[158] what happens if you release a cat in zero gravity – will it still twist? How would it know which way 'down' is to point its legs? If you were, then help is at hand. Experiments have taken place to answer just those questions. In 1947 the US Air Force took some cats up in Convair C-131 on what is known as a parabolic flight. Basically the plane ascends to a high

---

[157] Google 'cat righting reflex' to see an animation that demonstrates far more clearly than words can.

[158] 'May.' Probably not.

altitude and dives more or less straight down, creating around 30 seconds of weightlessness inside. These 'vomit comet' flights have been used for decades to train prospective astronauts for the experience of zero gravity in space. If you Google 'cats falling zero gravity' you can find some brief, but fairly incredible, footage of cats being released in zero-g. They are able, more or less, to twist their bodies around, although can end up pointing in different directions (and do not look very happy about the whole experience).

It may seem like a pretty pointless waste of time, jet fuel and cat happiness to establish something that, let's be honest, we would probably all have guessed at. Astonishingly though, studying falling cats turned out to be really very useful for NASA. The three-step process that a cat follows to self-right, whereby its front and back halves work as linked cylinders moving in opposite directions, was discovered by a pair of Stanford scientists in 1969. This research was used to help develop manoeuvres that astronauts could use to orientate themselves when floating free in space on space walks. Whatever you do, please don't attempt to test the ability of a cat to survive a fall. Even if it did get through the experience without a scratch it would be utterly terrifying for the animal.

Travelling cats

You may think that your cat is 'out of this world' but in the annals of human history there have only been two cats that literally have been out of this world. Or, to be more accurate, off this world. You will have probably heard about how dogs were sent into space, but you may be surprised to learn that two cats were sent up there as well. Félicette was one of 14 cats who were trained for space flight by the French as part of their space programme. The cats were obtained from a pet dealer, and (initially at least) not given names to help prevent the scientists becoming too attached to them.[159] All of the cats were female, and it was believed that they would be more relaxed about the whole affair than male cats would have been. The cats, rather unpleasantly, had electrodes surgically implanted in their brains to enable the researchers to monitor their brain activity

---

[159] I am not sure how well that would have worked, I don't need to know a cat's name to become attached to it. I just need to meet the cat.

while in space and underwent training that was akin to that humans would receive. They were placed in a high-g centrifuge, placed in a chair on gimbals while rocket noises were blasted at them, and put in small containers to acclimatise them to the confines of the capsule.

Félicette (at that point merely known as C341) was chosen to be the first cat in space, and on 18 October 1963 blasted skywards in an AGI 47 sounding rocket. After experiencing 9g of force, the puss finally reached a height of 152 km (94 miles) and experienced around five minutes of weightlessness before the capsule returned to Earth and was recovered. She managed to survive the experience with seemingly few ill effects; however, two months after her return from space she was euthanised by the scientists so that they could study her brain. A second cat, launched 11 days later, was even less fortunate. The nose cone of the rocket was badly damaged on landing and the cat died. In 2019 a statue memorialising Félicette was unveiled at the International Space University in eastern France, financed by a crowdfunding campaign. She stands tall and proud, on top of a globe, gazing up into space.

Another well-travelled cat who also had an unfortunate end was Mrs Chippy (confusingly a male cat), who was part of Sir Ernest Shackleton's ill-fated Imperial Trans-Antarctic Expedition of 1914-17. He was a particular favourite of the expedition's carpenter Harry 'Chippy' McNeish and acquired his name because he followed McNeish everywhere like an attentive wife. In 1915 the expedition's ship, the Endurance, became trapped in pack ice and was destroyed. Shackleton decided that they most humane thing to do was to kill the cat and the sled dogs swiftly, rather than have them suffer a long, drawn-out fate. Shackleton wrote in his diary on 29 October 1915:

> This afternoon Sallie's three youngest pups, Sue's Sirius, and Mrs. Chippy, the carpenter's cat, have to be shot. We could not undertake the maintenance of weaklings under the new conditions. Macklin, Crean, and the carpenter seemed to feel the loss of their friends rather badly.

In the case of Harry McNeish at least this seems to be something of an understatement. He never forgave Shackleton for the killing of his cat. McNeish had a troubled life after the expedition finally ended, in part due to the physical toll the conditions had taken upon his body. He died in New Zealand homeless and penniless at the age of 56 in 1930. Originally buried in an unmarked grave, he was finally given a headstone in 1959, and in 2004 a bronze statue of Mrs Chippy, happily sprawled out, was placed upon his tombstone. A man and his cat finally reunited in death. His grandson late said that this gesture would have meant more to McNeish than the Polar Medal he was awarded for his heroic expedition.

Nigel Cross

Harry McNeish and Mrs Chippy in life and death together

A number of cats have had arguably even more incredible journeys. There are numerous instances of cats travelling hundreds of miles to return to the place that they once lived. In 1977 a cat named Silky was lost by his owners a couple of hundred miles north of Brisbane in Australia. Around a year later the cat appeared at their home in Melbourne some 2,300 km (1,450 miles) away, thin and tired but otherwise in good shape. In 1981 a cat named Minosch travelled even further in much less time to get back to the comforts of home. He got out of his owner's vehicle at the Turkish border when the human was heading away for a holiday. Sixty-one days later there was a scratching at the door of the owner's house in Northern Germany some 2,400 km (1,500 miles) away and there was Minosch, home and almost certainly somewhat annoyed. Some people view these stories with a degree of skepticism – is it really *the same cat* who has appeared at the door? Or are their humans, missing their feline friend, making a forgivable assumption when a stray turns up at their door? Well, there have been cases where microchipped cats – so definitely the same creatures – have covered distances of 200 miles to return home, so there is some reason to believe that these stories are true.

How cats are able to navigate such incredible distances, across lands they have never visited before, to return home is something of a mystery. One theory is that cats are able to sense the magnetic field of the Earth, the myriad variations of which mean that it can be used as a kind of map. Alternatively (or indeed additionally) they are able to navigate using the stars. We just don't know for sure.

Political cats

You already know that Abraham Lincoln was a cat lover, but his were not the only 'First Kitties'. Bill Clinton had a cat named Socks, Woodrow Wilson had Puffins,[160] Gerald Ford and Jimmy Carter both brought Siamese cats to the White House and George W. Bush had a magnificent black beastie named Willie Bush. On the other side of the Atlantic, Winston Churchill was a noted cat lover, sharing Number 10 during the Second World War with Nelson. His affection for Nelson was recorded by the American war correspondent Quintin Reynolds, who recounts Churchill saying:

> Nelson is the bravest cat I ever knew. I once saw him chase a huge dog out of the Admiralty. I decided to adopt him and name him after our great Admiral...

Over the course of one dinner, Winston made sure that the cat was well fed:

---

[160] Yes, that is a very odd name for a cat. And indeed for anything other than a collection of puffins.

Churchill scarcely mentioned the war. Our first course was smoked salmon and twice, when Mrs. Churchill was not looking, the Prime Minister sneaked pieces of salmon to Nelson.

It has been said that his two great enemies, Hitler and Mussolini, not only didn't like cats they were actively afraid of them. There is a clinically recognised fear of cats *ailurophobia* (derived from the Greek words αἴλουρος (*ailouros*), 'cat', and φόβος (*phóbos*), 'fear') but quite how people come to develop this phobia is uncertain. As with dogs, an attack by a cat in early childhood may cause it to develop (though being attacked by a cat would generally be a lot less terrifying than an assault from a dog – at worst one would be likely to get a few scratches). Some people have a specific fear of big cats, which both makes a lot more rational sense and could possibly have a biological origin. When humans were hunter-gatherers big cats would likely have been our most common predators, so ensuring that we gave them a wide berth would be a useful trait for survival. Ailurophobia can be treated through what is termed 'exposure therapy' which involves, you guessed it, gradually exposing people to cats and through so doing demonstrating that there is nothing to fear. This can be done by first having someone play with a toy kitten, then after some time a real kitten, and finally end with encounters with a friendly cat.

A cat doesn't have to live with a politician to be political; they can actually be politicians themselves. There have been a surprising number of cats elected to office – though many of these have been purely ceremonial roles. Stubbs served as the mayor of the town of Talkeenta from his election in 1997 to his death in 2017. It should be noted that Stubbs didn't have any actual power in his role, but was much loved by the townspeople. Every afternoon he would pop into a local restaurant where he would be served a cocktail of water mixed with catnip, presented in a wine glass. In the late 1990s Catmando achieved arguably greater status by becoming the joint leader of the Official Monster Raving Loony Party (OMRLP).[161] After his tragically early death in a road accident at the age of seven, the OMRLP made it part of their formal manifesto that were they

---

[161] For those of you unfamiliar with British politics yes, this is a 'real' political party. No, they have never got anyone elected to anything.

ever elected to power they would pass a law forbidding any other cat to be named Catmando.

Hank the cat is a feline who actually ran for a contested human election (though he would not have been eligible to take up his seat were he elected. A loveable Maine Coon, he was put up for election in the 2012 US Senate election for the state of Virginia. Although he was a joke candidate his human campaign managers had a serious objective – raising awareness for rescue centres and animal groups. Hank spent election day fast asleep, but his human supporters stood outside polling stations attempting to drum up votes. As his name was (understandably) not on the actual ballot paper voters were forced to write in his name to show their support, and an amazing 7,319 did. While this was no where near enough to actually win the election, the campaign did manage to raise $60,000 for animal charities.

Larry, Chief Mouser to the Cabinet Office

In the UK there is a political cat with an official title: Chief Mouser to the Cabinet Office, which is bestowed upon the cat who lives with the Prime Minister at 10 Downing Street. There have been cats associated with the UK government for around 500 years, but the earliest known formal records date back to 3 June 1929 when formal authorisation was given to spend '1d[162] a day from petty cash towards the maintenance of an efficient cat'. This amount has increased and it is now apparently around £100 a year. This 'mouser in chief' is not necessarily owned by the Prime Minister – one incumbent, Wilderforce, served under four leaders between 1973 and 1986. For the last nine years the position has been held by Larry and the police officers guarding the door to the official residents can often be seen letting him in. Larry is held in such high esteem that Prime Minister David Cameron, in his final speech to Parliament before handing in his resignation to the Queen, made a point of confirming his affection for the beast:

> This gives me the opportunity to put a rumour to rest... this is the rumour that somehow I do not love Larry; I do, and I have photographic evidence to prove it. Sadly, I cannot take Larry with me; he belongs to the house and the staff love him very much, as do I.

At this point he pulled out a photograph of Larry sitting happily on his lap being fussed.

Working cats

'Working dogs' is a term that most people will recognise to describe support dogs, police dogs, sniffer dogs and so on. 'Working cats' is not an expression that you often hear being bandied around, but there have been large numbers of cats who have put in years of faithful service in a range of different roles. Unsurprisingly, many of them have been employed to keep rodent numbers under control. The Post Office in the UK has formally employed cats from 1868 until 1984 in just such roles; however, their employment has not been without controversy. In 1952 it was claimed that the cats had not received a pay rise since 1873, and a formal question was raised in the House of Commons to the Assistant Postmaster-General, David Gammans, 'When was the allowance payable for the maintenance of cats in his department last raised?' His slightly tongue-in-cheek response was as follows:

---

[162] 1d is basically a penny. But it doesn't quite convert, because at the time the UK had 240 pennies in each pound. Yes, not a nice round number like, say, 100. It may surprise you to discover that the change over to the decimal system of 100 pence in a pound only took place on 15 February 1971.

There is, I am afraid, a certain amount of industrial chaos in the Post Office cat world. Allowances vary in different places, possibly according to the alleged efficiency of the animals and other factors. It has proved impossible to organise any scheme for payment by results or output bonus. These servants of the State are, however, frequently unreliable, capricious in their duties and liable to prolonged absenteeism. My hon. and gallant Friend has been misinformed regarding the differences between rates for cats in Northern Ireland and other parts of the United Kingdom. There are no Post Office cats in Northern Ireland. Except for the cats at Post Office Headquarters who got the special allowance a few years ago, presumably for prestige reasons, there has been a general wage freeze since July, 1918, but there have been no complaints![163]

The most famous of the Post Office cats was Tibs the Great, who kept its London headquarters mouse free from 1950 till 1964 and was honoured with newspaper obituaries upon his death.

Cat-loving Japan has had its share of professional cats, the most famous of whom is Tama, the stationmaster cat. Originally a stray born in Kinokawa near Kishi station, she was adopted by a local at a

as365n2

---

[163] Yes, in the 'mother of all Parliaments' questions are asked – and answered – about the wages of cats.

time when the station was under threat of closure. In 2006, to save money, all station staff were made redundant, and local volunteers took on their roles. In 2007 Tama was officially awarded the title of 'Stationmaster' and given the role of greeting passengers upon their arrival. In reward for her labours she was given a bespoke hat and an annual supply of cat food. Such was her fame that passenger numbers to the station increased by 10%, and she is thought to have brought more than $10,000,000 in tourism revenues to the town. As the years passed she was further promoted, ultimately becoming 'Managing Executive Officer' of the rail company, and, technically, the third most senior manager in the business. In 2010 the station building was rebuilt to resemble a cat's face in her honour, and cat faces were painted on the trains. She died at the age of 16 in 2015 and was buried at a nearby Shinto shrine. Every year since on 23 June, the anniversary of her death, her cat successors visit the shrine, accompanied by the president of the rail company, to pay their respects to her.

One cat that earned a living not just for itself, but also for its owners was Blackie the Talking Cat. Carl and Elaine Miles would exhibit Blackie on the streets of Augusta, Georgia, and in return for a small sum of cash, the beastie would (allegedly) mew 'I love you' or 'I want my Mama'. Local police insisted that the Mileses get a $50 business licence to continue the venture, which the couple did, but then sued the city government on the basis the city charter did not specifically mention the need for a licence for a talking animal. Unsurprisingly, they lost the case. Surprisingly, they decided to appeal on the basis that Blackie's First Amendment right to free speech was being restricted. The appeal judges upheld the original ruling, noting:

> This Court will not hear a claim that Blackie's right to free speech has been infringed. First, although Blackie arguably possesses a very unusual ability, he cannot be considered a 'person' and is therefore not protected by the Bill of Rights. Second, even if Blackie had such a right, we see no need for appellants to assert his right jus tertii. Blackie can clearly speak for himself.

Another (non-working) cat who had a brush-in with the law is Lewis, a long-haired cat from Fairfield, Connecticut who was, err, placed under formal house arrest. Lewis had built up quite a reputation for attacking his human neighbours (and anyone else who happened to be in the vicinity). So much that a restraining order was taken out against him and he was placed under house arrest. His owner, Ruth Cisero, was unable to keep him inside, and was herself arrested for reckless engagement. Prosecutors offered to let her off with probation, but only if the cat were euthanised. Ruth refused, and chose to go to trial to save the life of her cat. Ultimately Lewis was spared, on the basis that he only left the house in future for trips to the vet, and then only in a cat carrier.

Many cats have served in the military, often in ceremonial roles, as mascots for companies of troops, but sometimes in more practical capacities. An amazing 500,000 cats were sent with British troops to fight in the trenches of the First World War. This was mostly, as was the case with the Roman army some 2,000 years earlier, to stop rats eating supplies, but they also provided an additional (if unpleasant) function. Due to their size, and their acute sense of smell, they would both become aware of, and suffer from ill effects from, gas attacks – they were essentially living gas detectors who could give a few precious seconds of additional warning to the troops that they served with. During the Second World War there were numerous reports of cats in London acting as a different kind of early warning system. Perhaps due to their ability to pick up the low drone of bomber aircraft before humans, they would lead families down into air-raid shelters before attacks took place.

In the middle of the 19th century Crimean Tom (also known as Sevastopol Tom) is said to have saved the lives of troops in a very different manner. In September 1855, during the Crimean War, French and British troops finally took the city of Sevastopol from the Russians after a year-long siege. After entering the city Lieutenant William Gair found Tom, dusty but otherwise unharmed, sitting on a pile of rubble and the two immediately took a shine to each other. The situation was harsh for the victorious troops though, as the siege had more or less exhausted the food supplies of the city and the soldiers were facing starvation. Gair noticed however that unlike the humans, who were getting thinner, Tom was getting fatter, and realised that he must have access to a ready supply of mice. Knowing that where there are mice there is going to a supply of food for mice, he followed the cat through the rubble one day and found an abandoned storeroom full of supplies.

It isn't just the military who have found roles for cats; spies have as well, but with not quite the success that they were looking for. 'Acoustic Kitty' was the name of a CIA programme which sounds as though it is the creation of a conspiracy theorist, but actually took place, as documents declassified in 2001 verified. During the Cold War the Americans were desperately trying to find ways to eavesdrop on their Russian counterparts and someone had the bright idea[164] of attempting to use cats. What follows isn't hugely pleasant for cats. After some years of research and experimentation they hit upon the scheme of implanting a microphone into the ear canal of the cat, and a radio transmitter at the base of its skull. The idea was that such cats could be released nearby Russian embassies and wander in, seeking food and human company. The Russians, having no idea that they had a spy in their midst, would continue to discuss their secret plans and all the while the Americans would be listening in. It has been claimed that the first attempted use of an acoustic kitty was to spy on two Russians in a park in Washington DC, and it was a total failure. Shortly after being released the cat was hit by a taxi and killed. Former CIA Director Robert Wallace went on the record in 2013 to disabuse the notion that the agency had caused the death of a cat in this manner saying *'the equipment was taken out of the cat; the cat was re-sewn for a second time, and lived a long and happy life afterwards'* and that the reason the programme was abandoned was that training cats to do what they wanted was simply too difficult. All told it is said that $20 million was spent trying to turn cats into spies.

Some cats have more artistic careers. If you have ever seen the film *Breakfast at Tiffany's* you will know that a pivotal role is played by Holly Golightly's cat, 'Cat' – or as she calls him 'a no-name slob'. The cat playing the role (quite magnificently) did of course have a name in real life, Orangey. This marmalade male feline had a

---

[164] Okay, not bright, bonkers.

career that many human actors would have been jealous of, appearing in TV shows and films for 16 years. He was particularly skilled at staying still for long periods of time[165] but was not always loved by his human co-stars. One studio executive said that he was 'the world's meanest cat' and would often bite or scratch his fellow performers. Sometimes, when he got fed up with the wonderful world of movie-making he would run away and hide, and the whole production would have be shut down until he could be found.

---

[165] This doesn't sound especially skilful. Most cats do this every day; it's called 'sleeping'.

Cats in the Wild

L
ater on I will be talking about some absolutely amazing domestic cats, but before I do I wanted to tell you a little bit about some of the wilder cousins of the domestic cat. Off the top of your head you can probably think of around ten different kinds of wild cat: lions, tigers, panthers, cougars, jaguars, cheetahs, wildcats, leopards, lynx, and so on. These broad names encompass most of the different types of cats, but in total there are 41 species of cats, that is to say members of the family Felidae that I mentioned earlier, and I am pretty sure that there are a fair few in there that you will never have heard of.[166]

The family *Felidae* is split into two sub-families, *Pantherinae* and *Felinae*. *Pantherinae* contains the five species that are generally called the 'big cats' – tiger, lion, jaguar, leopard and snow leopard. It also includes two other leopards, the clouded leopard and the Sunda clouded leopard.

Tigers are the largest living species of cat. Males range in total length from 250 to 390 cm (8.2 to 12.8 ft) and weigh between 90 and 300 kg (200 and 660 lb), with the largest recorded specimens reported at over 400 kg (880 pounds.) Females vary in total length from 200 to 275 cm (6.56 to 9.02 ft), and weigh 65 to 167 kg (143 to 368 lb). The tail accounts for around 0.6 to 1.1 m (2-3.5 feet) in both sexes.

They once roamed all across south and south-east Asia (including the islands of Java and Bali) as far west as modern-day Turkey, and up into temperate Siberian forests in the north. Human activity has, sadly, significantly reduced both the number and range of the tiger. The total global wild tiger population is today

---

[166] I hadn't heard of around a third of them. If you have heard of them all you are probably sufficiently expert that you can skip this section.

estimated to be around 4,000. Astonishingly (or perhaps not if you have watched *Tiger King*)[167] there are thought to be somewhere between 5,000 and 10,000 tigers living in captivity in the USA alone, with many more scattered in other countries around the world. Unfortunately many of these majestic beasts live in pretty terrible conditions, and even those that have decent open enclosures experience little of the life that they would have led in the outside world. Wild tigers have vast home ranges, anything from 50 km² (20 sq mi) to an astonishing 4,000 km² (1,500 sq mi).[168]

Charles J Sharp

Generally speaking tigers are solitary cats – they live and roam alone, and they hunt alone. They are also, interestingly, not particularly successful hunters: fewer than 10% of their attempts result in an actual kill. Lions, in contrast, are successful in making kills 17-19% of the time when they are hunting alone, and around 30% when they are hunting with other lions.

Moving on to **lions**, you probably think of them as beasts of the African savannah and forest – which is understandable, as other than a small population around the Gir National Park in Gujarat,

---

[167] Did you watch it? Through to the end? I got part-way through the first episode and found seeing those glorious cats so confined utterly depressing, so I stopped.
[168] Which is why I found *Tiger King* so depressing.

India, that is where all of the 20,000 or so wild lions live today. But that wasn't always the case; a few thousand years ago they would have covered the whole continent of Africa, the Middle East and a large swathe of South Asia. Indeed our old friend Herodotus reports that lions were frequently seen in Ancient Greece around 480 BC, though they sadly became extinct in that country over the course of the next 600 years.

Going back further into history, and you will find lions that roamed ever more widely across the world. *Panthera spelaea*, also known as the **Eurasian cave lion**, was a species of lion that emerged in Europe around half a million years ago. It covered a vast range across Europe, Russia, and the land bridge that then existed between Asia and North America into modern-day Alaska and Canada. Remains of this lion have even been found in England. It seems odd to think that a creature we now think of as being both rare and exotic was once commonplace in so much of the world.

A reconstruction of the North American lion

Panthera spelaea was somewhat larger than modern-day lions, but it was not the largest lion ever to exist. That title is held by *Panthera atrox* – the **North American lion**. They lived (unsurprisingly) in what is now the USA from around 340,000 years ago and only died out around 11,000 years ago and were huge cats – as quarter as large again as modern-day lions and weighing as much as half a tonne. Not only did they coexist with modern humans, there is evidence to suggest that we were responsible, at least in part, for their ultimate extinction – their bones have been found in ancient trash heaps of native Americans.

Cburnett

The third largest cat today is the **jaguar**; (above) most commonly thought of as jungle cats, they live across South America, up through Central America and Mexico and can occasionally be seen in Arizona, New Mexico and Texas. Their coats are dappled with distinctive black 'rosettes' which help to camouflage them in light-dappled trees. Solitary hunters, they excel at both swimming and tree climbing and are incredibly strong – they can drag a kill weighing many times their own weight up into a tree to protect it from other predators or flooding.

The final members of the *Panthera* sub-family are the **leopard** (*Panthera pardus*) and the **snow leopard** (*Panthera uncia*). Today leopards are found in sub-Saharan Africa, and in pockets across the Middle East, South and South-East Asia and on the island of Java, though they were (as with all large cats) once more widely dispersed and even lived in Japan.

Greg Hume

Snow leopards (above) live in the mountains of Central and South Asia, and have a strong claim to be the most beautiful of all wild cats (though that title is pretty hard to judge, I think!). They range across mountains and snow fields, living at altitudes of more than 6,000 metres (19,000 feet) in the summer months. The extreme climate of their territory means that they have very broad paws (to stop them sinking into the snow), thick fur and very fat tails. Literally very fat tails[169] – they use them to store fat – and they are also covered in a thick layer of fur so that the snow leopard can wrap it over its face while sleeping to help keep warm.

All of the other 36 species of cat – including the domestic cat – are members of the subfamily *Felinae*. Some of these species will be very well known to you, many of them though I suspect you will have never heard of.

Cheetah (*Acinonyx jubatus*)

As with many of the big cats, cheetahs could once be found in most of Africa, Asia and Europe but have become increasingly geographically limited through competition and the impact of humanity. Even as recently as the 1940s they could be found across much of

---

[169] I am not body-shaming snow leopards here!

Asia, from the Arabian peninsular through India and up into Asia. Now, other than a small population in Iran, they are only found in sub-Saharan Africa. Cheetahs are, of course, best known for their speed. We don't know exactly how fast they can run – estimates are 100-130 kph (60-80 mph) – but they are definitely the fastest land animal. A captive cheetah named Sarah from Cincinnati Zoo set a world record time for the 100 metres of 5.95 seconds, topping out at over 60 miles an hour. Given that she was a fairly elderly – 12 years old at the time (cheetahs in the wild typically live for 14-15 years) – it seems pretty likely that this is some way below the maximum possible speed for these beasts. Although they can run this quickly, during hunts they are only likely to reach 60-70% of their top speed, and even then only for a few seconds at time. This is because they burn an incredible amount of energy reaching and maintaining such a velocity – their breathing rate can hit 150 breaths per minute[170] – while their stride length can be as long as 7 metres (23 feet) with all four paws off the ground.

Unlike many species of wild cat, cheetahs can be easily tamed by humans and have been kept both as pets and hunters for at least 6,000 years, or perhaps even longer. Cave paintings in France from 30,000 years ago depict cheetahs, so it is possible that they were actually the first domesticated cats.

---

[170] If you (a human) are exercising *hard* you can expect to achieve a respiratory rate of around 50 breaths a minute, or roughly one a second. A cheetah can hit *three times* that.

Cougar (*Puma concolor*)

There are a number of cats that look like the cougar (below) – the **puma**, the **panther** and the **mountain lion** to name but a few. You may have wondered what the difference is between them. The answer is 'nothing': they are all the same species, just given different names in different places (and sometimes, confusingly, different names in the *same* place). This is something that the executives at the Ford Motor Company clearly weren't aware of – in the late 1990s they produced models called both the Cougar and the Puma, err, so both the same cat. Cougars can be found across all of South America, and as far north as Yukon in Canada. Unlike most other wild cats, cougars are not considered to be threatened and numbers are increasing in some areas, with there being an estimated 4-6,000 in California alone. Their wide geographic range has resulted in a vast array of prey species. In Patagonia, the southern tip of South America, they have been seen hunting penguins; in Florida one managed to kill an eight-foot-long alligator.

Art G

Related to the cougar, but much smaller, is the **jaguarundi** (*Herpailurus yagouaroundi*) which lives widely across South America, through Central America and Mexico, possibly once living in the USA. Long and slender and about twice the size of domestic cats, with long, muscular tails, they are excellent hunters and live across a wide range of habitats.

Eurasian lynx (*Lynx lynx*); **bobcat** (*Lynx rufus*); **Canada lynx** (*Lynx canadensis*) and the **Iberian lynx** (*Lynx pardinus*)
These four species make up the genus *Lynx*, medium-sized cats of similar appearance with distinctive tufts of black fur on the tips of their ears. They tend to live in mountainous forests, and are well adapted for living in cold climates, with thick winter coats and large paws (larger than a human hand), which allow them to walk upon snow without sinking. Often hunted for their pelts, there are huge variations in their numbers with the population of bobcats estimated at more than one million and that of the Iberian lynx being only 326 in 2012.

Black-footed cat (*Felis nigripes*)

This is the smallest wild cat in Africa, and is a little smaller than an average domestic cat. It is an incredibly cute cat,[171] but is almost the most deadly. Studied have found that around 60% of its hunts result in kills (tigers, you may remember, were doing well if they were successful one in ten times). It is a good thing that they are so successful at hunting: they need to eat a lot, around 15% of their body weight in prey each day. That's the equivalent of a human being eating 10 kg (22 pounds) of food. Black-footed cats aren't good at everything though – they are *terrible* at climbing trees (we've known a few domestic cats for whom that is also true, to be fair).

---

[171] Full disclosure – I think that most of these cats are incredibly cute.

Pallas's cat (*Otocolobus manul*)
Without wishing to sound like a massive egotist,[172] I would rather like to have a cat named after me, but we were born a couple of hundred years too late for that to have been a realistic possibility. Peter Simon Pallas was more fortunate, as in 1776 he got to name the cat that he discovered in eastern Siberia. Pallas's cat sits in a genus all on its own, is about the size of a domestic cat and lives in the steppes of Central Asia. It is a stocky kitty with short legs, very thick fur and a flattened head with small ears, which combine to give it an appearance of almost permanent discontent. It shouldn't be confused with...

Pampas cat (*Leopardus colocola*)
Slightly larger than the domestic cat, it lives in South America in forests and grasslands at altitudes between 1,800 and 5,000 metres (6,000 to 16,000 feet). Very little is known about this cat, and indeed there is considerable debate as to whether it is a single species of cat at all – a 2020 study suggested that there are actually five distinct species of pampas cat. (Perhaps it isn't too late to get a cat species named after us?) Very similar, both in appearance and range, to the pampas cat is the **Andean mountain cat** (*Leopardus jacobita*). Not a great deal is known about the Andean Mountain cat either. There are believed to be around 2,500 in the wild; however, the numbers are uncertain because they get confused with pampas cats. If you are ever in the Andes and spot a cat, the easiest way to tell the two apart is to count the rings on its tail. If it has fewer than nine rings, it *definitely* is an Andean cat. If it has *exactly* nine rings then, err, it is either an Andean cat or a Pampas cat. If the rings are wide, it is the former; if they are thin, the latter. I hope that this information comes in handy at some point for at least one of you.

---

[172] I do sound like one nonetheless.

Geoffroy's cat (*Leopardus geoffroyi*)

Yes, someone else get a species of cat named after them – this time it was Etienne Geoffroy Saint-Hilaire, a French zoologist who didn't discover the cat, but nonetheless had it named after him in 1844.[173] Geoffroy's cat is another cat native to South America and is about the size of a domestic cat.

Flat-headed cat (*Prionailurus planiceps*)

Jim Sanderson

We think that you are unlikely to have heard of this beast, easily identifiable due to, well, its flat head. Or, to be more precise, the depression of its skull. Roughly the size of a domestic cat, fewer than 2,500 remain living in the jungles of the Thai-Malay Peninsula and on the islands of Borneo and Sumatra. Little is known about these cats, and only a handful exist in captivity (where only three litters have been born). It is thought that these cats live almost exclusively on a diet of fish, which they catch by plunging their whole heads into the water then dragging their prey up the bank to stop it flapping back into the river. They have also been seen washing their food, in the much the same way that raccoons do. They are not alone in being expert in aquatic hunting, as is the ...

Fishing cat (*Prionailurus viverrinus*)

Fishing cats are members of the same genus as flat-headed cats, but are larger, almost twice the size of domestic cats. While their numbers are threatened, they cover a much larger geographic area and are found in a number of places across South and South-East

---

[173] Doesn't do the work, does get the credit. That is a handy skill to have.

Asia. As the name suggests, these are not kitties who are afraid of water. They are excellent swimmers and can even swim underwater, sometimes diving after fish.

Sunda leopard cat (*Prionailurus javanensis*) and the **leopard cat** (*Prionailurus bengalensis*)

These two species of cat are sufficiently similar in appearance that until 2017 they were considered to be the same species. About the size of a domestic cats, their markings are akin to those of leopards, hence their names. Leopard cats live across much of South-East Asia, as well as in southern India and up into northern Pakistan. Sadly they have long been hunted for their fur, with 200,000 a year being killed in China alone in the 1980s, though fewer are being slaughtered today. Archeological evidence from China suggests that they were living alongside humans, possibly as pets, as much as 5,000 years ago. The Sunda leopard cat lives on the Sundaland islands of South-East Asia (including Java, Sumatra and Borneo). Physically very similar to leopard cats, they are slightly smaller, and genetic analysis has found them to have diverged from the leopard cat a couple of hundred thousand years ago. The Bengal breed of cats is actually a cross-breed between the domestic cat and the leopard cat.

Rusty-spotted cat (*Prionailurus rubiginosus*)

This tiny feline vies with the black-footed cat for the title of smallest cat in the world. Significantly smaller than the domestic cat, it weighs only 0.9-1.6 kg (2-3.5 pounds). It lives across much of India, is active mostly at night, but other than that very little is known about its behaviour.

Ocelot (*Leopardus pardalis*) and **oncilla** (*Leopardus tigrinus*)

These two wild cats are somewhat similar in markings, but differ in size. The ocelot lives across northern South America, Central America and up into the south-western states of the USA. Several times the size of a domestic cat, it is a highly successful hunter that likes to live in thick vegetation, close to water. Like so many other species of cat the ocelot was intensely hunted for its fur – with as many of 140,000 of the cats being traded each year in the 1960s. Things have improved somewhat thanks to a number of countries banning the trade in their skins, and some 40,000 are believed to live in the wild today. From time to time they are tamed and kept as pets, and tend to be both highly affectionate and demanding of attention. Perhaps the most famous owner of an ocelot was the artist Salvador Dali, who travelled with his pet Babou.[174] On one occasion he took the cat out to dinner with him to a restaurant in New York and reassured an alarmed diner that it was not a wild beast; rather, he said, it was a domestic cat he had painted as a piece of art. Given that ocelots can weight more than 15 kg (33 pounds) I am not sure how convincing this explanation would have been.[175] Oncillas are much closer in size to domestic cats – somewhat slimmer and longer, but roughly the same weight. They live primarily in the Amazon basin, though populations do exist in Costa Rica and Panama and up into the Andes. Oncillas have been known to naturally cross-breed with both pampas cats and Geoffroy's cat. Sadly I haven't been able to find a picture of an oncilla/pampas cross – I would love to see one as they are so different in appearance!

The southern tiger cat or southern tigrina (*Leopardus guttulus*)
This is another close relative of the oncilla, and indeed was considered to be a sub-species of it for many years. It too cross-breeds with Geoffroy's cat and lives in dense forests in Brazil, Paraguay and Argentina. It is so similar to the oncilla that it is basically impossible to tell the two cats apart by looking at them – you need to carry out genetic analysis to figure out which is which. Sadly, it too used to be widely hunted for its fur and is now threatened as a result.

---

[174] Do Google for pictures of Babou, it is a *glorious* cat. It probably would have been happier in the wild though. Sigh.

[175] Um, not convincing *at all* I suspect. It is entirely possible that this story is just made up, even though it is widely reported. Fake news!

Margay (*Leopardus wiedii*)

When it comes to cats I really don't like to pick favourites, but if I *had* to then I would probably choose the margay. Like the oncilla, it has very similar markings to the ocelot but is much closer in size to a long domestic cat. it is probably the best climber in the cat kingdom; some margays are thought to spend their entire lives in the trees of Central and South America hunting birds and monkeys. It is sufficiently strong and agile that researchers have seen it hanging from a branch by just one paw. It also has the

Supreet Sahoo

ability to climb down trees face first. This might not seem particularly special, but have you ever wondered why domestic cats, having scrambled up a tree trunk, scrabble down tail first? The answer is that they cannot turn their ankles sufficiently to climb down forwards – they would simply fall off if they tried. Only the margay and the clouded leopard are able to manage this.

Kodkod (*Leopardus guigna*)

The name may make it sound like it is a pair of fish, but the kodkod is actually the smallest of the South American cats, a little smaller than a domestic cat with big feet and a thick tail. They live in temperate rainforests in the foothills of, and plains around, the Andes. Not a great deal is known about them – there are believed to be 10,000 in the wild and are under threat. No kodkods are currently kept in zoos, though there is a project in Chile that is attempting to breed them which has a couple of individuals. It has been reported that local people believed kodkods to be vampires, as the bite marks left by their canines on the necks of unfortunate chickens looked as though a mythic beast had been draining their blood.

Caracal (*Caracal caracal*), **serval** (*Leptailurus serval*) and **African golden cat** (*Caracal aurata*)

Caracals are medium-sized cats with a combined body and tail length of over 1.4 metres (more than 4 feet) and can weigh as much as 20 kg (44 pounds). They have plain, sandy-coloured bodies with very distinctive black tufts on the tips of their ears. They can be found across sub-Saharan Africa, the Arabian Peninsula and across into India and Central Asia. They are one of the species of cat that was tamed and used as hunters by the Ancient Egyptians. The African golden cat is a close relative, and is of similar size; however, its coat is very different. You may have thought that, given its name, its coat would be golden, but these 'golden' cats come a range of colours, grey, chestnut, reddish brown, and almost black. They can be plain, they can be spotted. They are yet another species of cat about whom, due to their reclusive behaviour, not a great deal is known. Both are also closely related to the serval, a somewhat more 'traditional' looking cat with a golden-yellow coat covered in black spots and stripes. Servals are particularly noteworthy because in the late 1980s they were successfully bred with domestic cats to create the savannah cat breed. Savannah cats are the large breed of 'domestic' cat (technically they *are* domestic cats, but it feels a little odd to me to call a cross between a wild cat and a domestic cat truly domestic) and can weigh more than 9 kg (20 pounds). Long and lithe, they are exceptionally good jumpers, loyal and friendly (they will often follow their humans around much as a dog would do) and unlike most domestic cats *love* water.

Asian golden cat (*Catopuma temminckii*)

Despite having a very similar name to the African Golden Cat, the Asian golden cat is actually somewhat of a distant relative; it is actually much more closely related to the **bay cat** (*Catopuma badia*). The Asian golden cat is also known as Temminck's cat (as its Latin name suggests), being named after the Dutch zoologist Coenraad Jacob Temminck.[176] The Asian golden cat is a medium-sized beast that lives across northeastern India, South-East Asia and southern China and,

---

[176] Yes, someone else got a cat named after them, and no, Temminick didn't discover the cat, he was just a big cheese in Dutch zoology in the first half of the 19th century.

sadly like so many other wild cats, is under threat as its natural habitat becomes increasingly encroached upon by humans. The bay cat is in even greater danger, with only around 2,500 of the creatures remaining on the island of Borneo. Even by the standards of rare and secretive cats, very little is known about the bay cat. The first one was captured alive in *1992* and since then there have been only isolated sightings and records from camera traps. It is unusual in that it has bright, chestnut reddish fur, not dissimilar to the red fox.

Sand cat (*Felis margarita*)

Charles Barilleaux

We have heard a lot about small species of wild cats that live in forests. The sand cat is very different indeed. This little beastie lives (as you might have guessed from the name) in the harsh, arid deserts of north Africa, the Middle East, and central Asia. About the size of a domestic cat they are, yes, incredibly cute. Their paws have to cope with ground temperatures that are so hot during the day that they would blister human skin, and so cold at night that they can drop below freezing point. To achieve this, fur grows out from between their toes, forming a pad under the paw to protect it (and having the side effect of making their tracks hard to follow). Their hearing is incredibly sensitive, due to having ear canals twice the size of a domestic cat, which means that they can hear sounds around that are around an eighth the volume. They live in burrows under the sand during the day in summer in order to escape the heat, taking over ones abandoned by other animals such as porcupines. While they will readily drink water if it is available, they don't need to, as they can obtain all of their moisture needs from their prey of rodents and snakes.

Jungle cat (*Felis chaus*)
The jungle cat in contrast *loves* wetlands and for this reason is known as the 'reed cat' or 'swamp cat'. A medium-sized cat (it can weigh 16 kg / 35 pounds) it lives across a broad swathe of central and south Asia and across into the wetlands of South-East Asia and it has been seen as high as 3,300 metres (10,000 feet) in the mountains of Nepal. Perhaps unsurprisingly, given its name, this is a cat that is very comfortable in the water, swimming for up to a mile at a time and diving underwater to hunt fish.

African wildcat (*Felis lybica*)
The African wildcat, I have said earlier, is the species of cat known to have cohabited with humans the earliest, from the 9,500-year-old grave site in Cyprus. Not much larger than the domestic cat (to which they are closely related and can cross-breed with) they live across Africa and west Asia. Thankfully (and perhaps surprisingly) they are not a threatened species at all.

Lviatour

European wildcat (*Felis silvestris*)
The European wildcat once would have roamed across the whole continent but now lives in a range of pockets including Spain, parts of Italy and Turkey, and a small population in Scotland in the UK. The Scottish population separated from the rest when rising sea levels after the last period of glaciation turned Britain back into an island. They would have once lived all over England, Scotland

and Wales; however, the interventions of humans (particularly gamekeepers) steadily led to their decline. They were wiped out of southern England about 500 years ago, in Wales and northern England by the middle of the 19th century, and now only survive in northern Scotland. They readily breed with domestic cats, a fact which is threatening their population still further. Excitingly[177] there is a plan to reintroduce European wildcats back into the wild in England by 2022. Despite their physical and genetic similarity to domestic cats, European wildcats are reputed to be basically impossible to tame and keep as pets, though as I have mentioned before, crosses between wildcats and domestic cats are much more amenable towards humans.

Chinese mountain cat (*Felis bieti*)

Finally[178] there is the newest cat species – though to be clear when I say 'newest' in this context I don't mean the species most recent to evolve, rather to be classified as a distinct species by humans. It was only 2017 that the Chinese mountain cat was formally recognised as a valid species, separate from other wildcats. Until recently all of our knowledge about these felines came from six cats living in zoos in China, and a few preserved skins. Then in May 2007 one was photographed in the wild for the first time, caught in a camera trap trotting through the snow at 3,570 metres (almost 12,000 feet) in Sichuan. As you may have guessed we really don't know very much about these cats; they are small-medium sized, weighing up to 9 kg (20 pounds) and have thick fur (including a magnificent tail) to help protect them from the elements. They live at altitudes of up to 5,000 metres (16,400 feet) and live on birds and small mammals.

---

[177] Exciting if you like wildcats, that is.
[178] I *think* that we have mentioned them all now.

Alien Big Cats

Alien big cats (ABCs), also known as phantom cats, are neither (you may be disappointed to learn) huge cats that have landed from outer space, nor are they ghost cats. What they actually are is members of large cat species such as jaguars, cougars and leopards that are *believed* to be living outside of their indigenous range. Basically, it is a large cat living somewhere where, by the laws of nature, it has no right to be. There are many, many stories about ABCs but very little actual evidence to suggest that they really exist. For more than 100 years there have been reports of exotic big cats living in the wild in Australia. In Gippsland there are said to live cougars who were bought over as mascots by US airmen during the Second World War and then released into the bush.[179] The Blue Mountains Panther has been reported as living in the Blue Mountains near Sydney for more than 100 years, with more than 500 reported sightings in the last 20 years alone. It too is said to have said to have been descended from mascots released by US airmen, or perhaps escapees of travellings circuses. In 2002 a teenager was even attacked by what he claimed was the beast, and in 2011 a pet alpaca was killed by *something* that could have been a big cat. Footage of a large cat was captured on video and examined by experts, but they concluded that it was simply a very large domestic cat.

There have been thousands of reported sightings of big cats in the wild in the UK over the years, and to be fair there have been a number of cases where large cats have escaped from captivity and subsequently been killed or recaptured. What there hasn't been is any conclusive evidence of such animals living sustainably in the wild. One of the most famous cases is the Beast of Bodmin Moor, a large black cat said to live on, you guessed it, Bodmin Moor in Cornwall. The rumours of big cats roaming free on the moor have been around for more than 40 years. They were seemingly proven to be well founded in 1995 when the actual skull of a young male leopard was found by a river. Analysis showed however that it has

---

[179] Why would they got to the trouble of bringing them thousands of miles only to release them? Also, these were their mascots, right? Surely they would want to keep, you know, 'mascotting'.

been taken from a leopard skin rug, and that the egg case from a tropical cockroach found inside the skull proved that the cat had died outside the UK. Coincidentally the skull was found only a week[180] after an official government report found no evidence of exotic felines on the loose in the country. Less well known, the Charlbury Panther is said to roam the woodlands of Oxfordshire. It seems likely however that most of these 'sightings' are people spotting a black metal sculpture of a panther created by a local artist.

The vast and largely empty (of humans) wilderness areas in Australia do make it seem at least somewhat possible that there are as yet undiscovered groups of escaped big cats living there. However as these animals could only have been descended from a relatively small number of initial escapees the gene pool would be extremely limited, leading to genetic problems as they inbred over the generations. In the UK, particularly the south of England which is fairly densely populated and has no real areas of true wilderness, the claims seem rather more absurd. For these animals to have survived for decades with no bodies being found, and no decent footage being taken of them, rather defies belief. It is particularly strange that now almost everyone has a fairly high quality camera in their smartphone that we don't have a slew of pictures suddenly being taken.

Extinct Cats

We have already talked about some cat species that are now extinct. Some of them became extinct very recently indeed, thanks, yes, to the activities of humans. The Barbary lion lived in North Africa until being declared extinct in the 1960s. Originally thought to have been a sub-species of lion, DNA analysis in 2017 found that they were actually a distinct species in their own right, albeit one that we had wiped out around 40 years earlier. There are dozens more species of cat known to have once lived and doubtless dozens more that we know nothing about. Probably the most famous are the sabre-toothed cats, readily identified by the long, curved, sabre-like teeth that protruded from their mouths. These fearsome felines were found pretty much everywhere around the world (apart from

---

[180] That is very convenient timing, isn't it?

Australia) until around 11,000 years ago. More than 50 species of these cats existed, spread across a large number of genera. The best known of these is *Smilodon*, commonly known as the sabre-toothed tigers, though truth be told they are not that closely related to tigers (or, indeed, and other species of modern cat). Three species are currently recognised, ranging in size from *Smilodon gracilis* which weighed up to 100 kg (220 pounds) to the massive *Smilodon populator* which could be more than 430 kg (950 pounds) or almost half a tonne. That makes them almost half as large again (in weight terms) as tigers, the largest of the extant cats.

A sabre-toothed tiger, as imagined by Charles R. Knight in 1903

Sabre-toothed tigers lived across North and South America, and we know from analysis of their bones that they even more powerfully built than living cats.[181] As for those famous teeth, in *Smilodon populator* they were around 28 cm – almost a foot – long. It is incredible to believe that these creatures once lived in the same places as modern humans, but they did, becoming extinct around 10,000 years ago. The exact cause of their extinction is unclear, and while you may have seen pictures of fur-clad cave people hurling flint-tipped spears at such beasts, it seems unlikely that hunting by humans caused them to disappear. For one thing, they are likely to have been very hard to kill indeed, and even attempting to do so would have carried enormous risk for the humans involved.

A more accepted view is that humans did lead to their extinction,

---

[181] I don't know about you, but the notion of a cat half as big again as a tiger, even stronger and with massive sabre teeth is *just a little bit frightening*.

but not directly. At around the same time many *megaherbivores* (massive, plant-eating animals like the woolly mammoth) became extinct, possibly hunted into nothing by hungry humans. With their main sources of food gone the cats found it difficult to survive and disappeared shortly afterwards. This hypothesis is not universally accepted though. It has been pointed out that other large herbivores were widely hunted for food until the last century, and survived just fine. There is also a very practical point: a mammoth would have weighed 5-6 tonnes, and a typical hunter-gatherer tribe would have likely contained no more than 100 people. If they succeeded in bringing down one of these vast beasts that would mean around 50 kg (110 pounds) of meat per person. Now in the middle of winter you may have been able to keep that fresh (though would have had to protect it from scavengers) but as soon as temperatures rose much about freezing it would have quickly spoiled. It would be far less wasteful (and easier from a hunt perspective) to take down a smaller animal such as an elk instead.

Another theory suggests that the cause was climate change. The planet was moving out of a period of glaciation at time, and as temperatures increased (really quite rapidly) so the vegetation would have changed, potentially threatening the herbivores. Higher temperatures would have also increased the risk of fire, a problem made worse by the fact that fire-creating humans had recently moved to the continent. A final way that humans could have been to blame is through spreading novel diseases to the continent when we arrived. The honest answer is though that we will probably never be sure about the exact cause.

Cats in Literature

Given how effectively cats have slunk their way into myths and folklore, it is perhaps not unsurprising that they should also appear fairly frequently in works of literature. Sometimes they are little more than background decoration – something for the protagonist to stroke or have concern about. At other times they have agency of their own, playing a pivotal role in the story. (A standard textbook for Hollywood screenwriters these days is *Save the Cat!* By Blake Snyder, the idea being that when the hero does something like save a cat, they are worth rooting for.)[182] Sometimes cats in stories are even imbued with human characteristics and sentience, either implicitly or explicitly. The fondness of writers for featuring cats in their creative output is likely not simply because of their intriguing feline properties; quite a lot of successful writers simply *love* cats. As writing is a fairly lonely task, having a puss around, curled nearby in a puddle of sunshine, can be a source of great companionship as one grinds out the words. Of course as anyone who has lived with cats will attest, it can also be a source of great distraction, particularly when the cat decides that the best place in the world to sit is on your keyboard.

Probably the most famous cat in literature is the Cheshire Cat, from *Alice's Adventures in Wonderland* by Lewis Carroll. While he created the character of the Cheshire Cat, the concept of a grinning Cheshire feline had been around for some years. The 1788 book *A Classical Dictionary of the Vulgar Tongue* includes the entry:

> **Cheshire cat.** *He grins like a Cheshire cat*; said of any one who shows his teeth and gums in laughing.

---

[182] Well duh.

A decade before *Alice* was published William Makepeace Thackeray used the expression in his novel *The Newcomes*: 'That woman grins like a Cheshire cat.'

The origin of the expression, the people of Cheshire often claim, is that their cats are seen to grin so happily because of the wonderful cream and milk produced by local dairy farms. In 1853 the writer Samuel Maunder proposed a different (and to my mind somewhat tenuous) alternative explanation:

> This phrase owes its origin to the unhappy attempts of a sign painter of that country to represent a lion rampant, which was the crest of an influential family, on the sign-boards of many of the inns. The resemblance of these lions to cats caused them to be generally called by the more ignoble name. A similar case is to be found in the village of Charlton, between Pewsey and Devizes, Wiltshire. A public-house by the roadside is commonly known by the name of The Cat at Charlton. The sign of the house was originally a lion or tiger, or some such animal, the crest of the family of Sir Edward Poore.

As to why Carroll included the cat in his book the answer may, surprisingly, be mathematical. The term 'catenary' is given to describe the curve made by a horizontally suspended chain, a very grin-like shape. This gave rise to the riddle:

Riddle: What kind of a cat can grin?
Answer: A Catenary.[183]

---

[183] OK, perhaps not one to have you rolling on the floor with laughter.

As Carroll was a mathematician at the University of Oxford is it quite possible that this was the inspiration for his smiling moggie. Carroll seems to have been a cat lover, and he describes the contrary nature of the beasts quite wonderfully in *Alice*:

> And how do you know that you're mad? [asked Alice] 'To begin with,' said the Cat, 'a dog's not mad. You grant that?' I suppose so, said Alice. 'Well then,' the Cat went on, 'you see a dog growls when it's angry, and wags its tail when it's pleased. Now I growl when I'm pleased, and wag my tail when I'm angry. Therefore I'm mad.'

Another contender for the most famous cat in literature (though, I suspect, rather less well-known today than the riddling, smiling Wonderland creature) is Jeoffry, the cat who belonged to the 18th century poet Christopher Smart. A 74-line section of this religious poem *Jubilate Agno* is dedicated to his pet, praising both the puss and its relationship with God:

> For I will consider my Cat Jeoffry.
> For he is the servant of the Living God duly and daily serving him.
> For at the first glance of the glory of God in the East he worships in his way.
> For this is done by wreathing his body seven times round with elegant quickness.
> For then he leaps up to catch the musk, which is the blessing of God upon his prayer.
> For he rolls upon prank to work it in.
> For having done duty and received blessing he begins to consider himself.
> For this he performs in ten degrees.
> For first he looks upon his forepaws to see if they are clean.
> For secondly he kicks up behind to clear away there.
> For thirdly he works it upon stretch with the forepaws extended.
> For fourthly he sharpens his paws by wood.
> For fifthly he washes himself.
> For sixthly he rolls upon wash.
> For seventhly he fleas himself, that he may not be interrupted upon the beat.
> For eighthly he rubs himself against a post.

For ninthly he looks up for his instructions.

For tenthly he goes in quest of food.

For having consider'd God and himself he will consider his neighbour.

For if he meets another cat he will kiss her in kindness.

For when he takes his prey he plays with it to give it a chance.[184]

For one mouse in seven escapes by his dallying.

For when his day's work is done his business more properly begins.

For he keeps the Lord's watch in the night against the adversary.

For he counteracts the powers of darkness by his electrical skin and glaring eyes.

For he counteracts the Devil, who is death, by brisking about the life.

For in his morning orisons he loves the sun and the sun loves him.

For he is of the tribe of Tiger.

For the Cherub Cat is a term of the Angel Tiger.

For he has the subtlety and hissing of a serpent, which in goodness he suppresses.

For he will not do destruction, if he is well-fed, neither will he spit without provocation.

For he purrs in thankfulness, when God tells him he's a good Cat.

For he is an instrument for the children to learn benevolence upon.

For every house is incomplete without him and a blessing is lacking in the spirit.

For the Lord commanded Moses concerning the cats at the departure of the Children of Israel from Egypt.

For every family had one cat at least in the bag.[185]

For the English Cats are the best in Europe.

For he is the cleanest in the use of his forepaws of any quadruped.

For the dexterity of his defence is an instance of the love of God to him exceedingly.

For he is the quickest to his mark of any creature.

For he is tenacious of his point.

For he is a mixture of gravity and waggery.

For he knows that God is his Saviour.

For there is nothing sweeter than his peace when at rest.

---

[184] No, he is just playing with it, it isn't some kind of opportunity for merciful escape

[185] Do they? If so could they please *let the cat out of the bag!*

For there is nothing brisker than his life when in motion.

For he is of the Lord's poor and so indeed is he called by benevolence perpetually—Poor Jeoffry! poor Jeoffry! the rat has bit thy throat.

For I bless the name of the Lord Jesus that Jeoffry is better.

For the divine spirit comes about his body to sustain it in complete cat.

For his tongue is exceeding pure so that it has in purity what it wants in music.

For he is docile and can learn certain things.

For he can set up with gravity which is patience upon approbation.

For he can fetch and carry, which is patience in employment.

For he can jump over a stick which is patience upon proof positive.

For he can spraggle upon waggle at the word of command.

For he can jump from an eminence into his master's bosom.

For he can catch the cork and toss it again.

For he is hated by the hypocrite and miser.

For the former is afraid of detection.

For the latter refuses the charge.

For he camels his back to bear the first notion of business.

For he is good to think on, if a man would express himself neatly.

For he made a great figure in Egypt for his signal services.

For he killed the Ichneumon-rat very pernicious by land.

For his ears are so acute that they sting again.

For from this proceeds the passing quickness of his attention.

For by stroking of him I have found out electricity.

For I perceived God's light about him both wax and fire.

For the Electrical fire is the spiritual substance, which God sends from heaven to sustain the bodies both of man and beast.

For God has blessed him in the variety of his movements.

For, tho he cannot fly, he is an excellent clamberer.

For his motions upon the face of the earth are more than any other quadruped.

For he can tread to all the measures upon the music.

For he can swim for life.

For he can creep.

There is clearly quite a lot to unpack in there, and, for sure, lots of things I would agree with in terms of cat behaviour (and, indeed the history of cats) but love them as I do, I don't think that it is really fair to say that 'English Cats are the best in Europe'. Nor have I ever seen a cat 'spraggle upon waggle[186] at the word of command'. It also does seem that he is perhaps reaching somewhat when he interprets what appears to be just regular cat behaviour as somehow reflecting its reverence for god. It is perhaps worth mentioning that when he wrote the poem, Smart was confined to St Luke's Hospital for Lunatics.

The other great poetic puss is Edward Lear's beast, who has a starring role in 'The Owl and the Pussy-cat':

The Owl and the Pussy-cat went to sea
In a beautiful pea-green boat,
They took some honey, and plenty of money,
Wrapped up in a five-pound note.
The Owl looked up to the stars above,
And sang to a small guitar,
'O lovely Pussy! O Pussy, my love,
        What a beautiful Pussy you are,
    You are,
    You are!
What a beautiful Pussy you are!'

Pussy said to the Owl, 'You elegant fowl!
How charmingly sweet you sing!
O let us be married! too long we have tarried:
But what shall we do for a ring?'
They sailed away, for a year and a day,
To the land where the Bong-Tree grows
And there in a wood a Piggy-wig stood
With a ring at the end of his nose,
        His nose,
        His nose,
    With a ring at the end of his nose.

'Dear Pig, are you willing to sell for one shilling
Your ring?' Said the Piggy, 'I will.'

---

[186] If you have any idea what 'spraggle upon waggle' actually *means* then please let me know; the best answer will win the prize of my undying respect.

So they took it away, and were married next day
By the Turkey who lives on the hill.
They dined on mince, and slices of quince,
Which they ate with a runcible spoon;
And hand in hand, on the edge of the sand,
They danced by the light of the moon,
> The moon,
> The moon,
They danced by the light of the moon.

Lear himself was crazy about cats, and besotted with his companion Foss, who was the model for the pussycat in the poem and often drawn by Lear. Foss would 'help' Lear as he worked by rolling on his manuscripts to dry the ink (the 19th century equivalent of sitting on a laptop, I think). So concerned was Lear about the happiness of his cat that when he moved towns in Italy he got his architect to build a new villa with exactly the same layout as his old home so that Foss wouldn't get confused when they

moved. Despite this, the story goes, on the first day in his new home Foss climbed up a chimney to hide. That sounds like the kind of thing pretty much every cat I have ever met would do.

Charles Dickens didn't really write very much about cats. Other than one puss who plays a minor role in *Bleak House* they are only mentioned as background scenery. There is a pretty good reason to think that he was fond of cats though. Okay, perhaps not a *good* reason. More like a *downright freaking weird and macabre* reason. Dickens, you see, had a cat letter-opener. Not a letter-opener shaped like a cat or decorated with cats. No. A letter-opener *made* from a cat. From the stuffed paw of his pet cat 'Bob' to be precise. Of course the paw on its own wasn't going to be much use for opening letters; it was used as the handle of an ivory blade upon which was inscribed 'C.D. In Memory of Bob 1862'. Awww. Sweet. Or weird. Your choice. There is actually another reason to believe that Dickens loved cats, and that comes from a story told by his daughter Mamie:

> On account of our birds, cats were not allowed in the house; but from a friend in London I received a present of a white kitten — Williamina — and she and her numerous offspring had a happy home at 'Gad's Hill.' ... As the kittens grow older they became more and more frolicsome, swarming up the curtains, playing about on the writing table and scampering behind the bookshelves. But they were never complained of and lived happily in the study until the time came for finding them other homes. One of these kittens was kept, who, as he was quite deaf, was left unnamed, and became known by servants as 'the master's cat,' because of his devotion to my father. He was always with him, and used to follow him about the garden like a dog, and sit with him while he wrote. One evening we were all, except father, going to a ball, and when we started, left 'the master' and his cat in the drawing-room together. 'The master' was reading at a small table, on which a lighted candle was placed. Suddenly the candle went out. My father, who was much interested in his book, relighted the candle, stroked the cat, who was looking at him pathetically he noticed, and continued his reading. A few minutes later, as the light became dim, he looked up just in time to see puss deliberately put out the candle with his paw, and then look appealingly towards him. This second and unmistakable hint was not disregarded, and puss was given the petting he craved. Father was full of this anecdote when all met at breakfast the next morning.

Now we know cats try all kind of things to get a bit of attention and a friendly stroke but Bob, putting out a lit candle with his paw? That is seriously Champion's League level stuff.

Edgar Allan Poe, the master of mystery stories, wrote a tale entitled 'The Black Cat' in which the (really very unpleasant) narrator tells of how his initial affection for his cat wanes and he treats it with terrible cruelty (if you don't like to read about something nasty being done to a cat please feel free to skip this section).

Pluto—this was the cat's name—was my favorite pet and playmate. I alone fed him, and he attended me wherever I went about the house. It was even with difficulty that I could prevent him from following me through the streets.

Our friendship lasted, in this manner, for several years, during which my general temperament and character—through the instrumentality of the Fiend Intemperance—had (I blush to confess it) experienced a radical alteration for the worse. I grew, day by day, more moody, more irritable, more regardless of the feelings of others. I suffered myself to use intemperate language to my wife. At length, I even offered her personal violence. My pets, of course, were made to feel the change in my disposition. I not only neglected, but ill-used them. For Pluto, however, I still retained sufficient regard to restrain me from maltreating him, as I made no scruple of maltreating the rabbits, the monkey, or even the dog, when by accident, or through affection, they came in my way. But my disease grew upon me—for what disease is like Alcohol!—and at length even Pluto, who was now becoming old, and consequently somewhat peevish—even Pluto began to experience the effects of my ill temper.

One night, returning home, much intoxicated, from one of my haunts about town, I fancied that the cat avoided my presence. I seized him; when, in his fright at my violence, he inflicted a slight wound upon my hand with his teeth. The fury of a demon instantly possessed me. I knew myself no longer. My original soul seemed, at once, to take its flight from my body and a more than fiendish malevolence, gin-nurtured, thrilled every fibre of my frame. I took from my waistcoat-pocket a pen-knife, opened it, grasped the poor beast by the throat, and deliberately cut one of its eyes from the socket![187] I blush, I burn, I shudder, while I pen the damnable atrocity.

Things sadly get worse for the cat from there. The narrator ends up killing the poor beast by hanging it from a tree in the garden. Or (spoiler!) *does he really kill it?* He goes on to kill his wife and her

---

[187] I DID WARN YOU!

zombie corpse appears when the police turn up... and on her head 'sat the hideous beast whose craft had seduced me into murder'. Charming stuff.

There have been many writers who clearly 'get' cats, and I would like to share some of my favourite passages by them:

> Throw a stick, and the servile dog wheezes and pants and stumbles to bring it to you. Do the same before a cat, and he will eye you with coolly polite and somewhat bored amusement. And just as inferior people prefer the inferior animal which scampers excitedly because someone else wants something, so do superior people respect the superior animal which lives its own life and knows that the puerile stick-throwings of alien bipeds are none of its business and beneath its notice. The dog barks and begs and tumbles to amuse you when you crack the whip. That pleases a meekness-loving peasant who relishes a stimulus to his self importance. The cat, on the other hand, charms you into playing for its benefit when it wishes to be amused; making you rush about the room with a paper on a string when it feels like exercise, but refusing all your attempts to make it play when it is not in the humour. That is personality and individuality and self-respect — the calm mastery of a being whose life is its own and not yours — and the superior person recognises and appreciates this because he too is a free soul whose position is assured, and whose only law is his own heritage and aesthetic sense. [188]
>
> **– H. P. Lovecraft**

> Having a bunch of cats around is good. If you're feeling bad, just look at the cats, you'll feel better, because they know that everything is, just as it is.
>
> **– Charles Bukowski, *On Cats***

> I'd take cyanide no problem if it was that or throwing a cat out in the street, even a moth-eaten, mangy, caterwauling pain in the ass! I'd rather have the thing in bed with me than see it suffer on my account... though when it comes to human beings, I'm only

---

[188] I love dogs as well, and have to say that this passage is really a bit unfair on them, even if it is great about cats.

interested in the sick... the ones who can stand up are nothing but mounds of vice and spite... I don't get mixed up in their schemes...
– **Louis-Ferdinand Céline**, *Normance*

What sort of philosophers are we, who know absolutely nothing of the origin and destiny of cats?[189]
– **Henry David Thoreau**, *Journal 9*

That's the way with a cat, you know — any cat; they don't give a damn for discipline. And they can't help it, they're made so. But it ain't really insubordination, when you come to look at it right and fair — it's a word that don't apply to a cat. A cat ain't ever anybody's slave or serf or servant, and can't be — it ain't in him to be. And so, he don't have to obey anybody. He is the only creature in heaven or earth or anywhere that don't have to obey somebody or other, including the angels. It sets him above the whole ruck, it puts him in a class by himself. He is independent. You understand the size of it? He is the only independent person there is. In heaven or anywhere else. There's always somebody a king has to obey — a trollop, or a priest, or a ring, or a nation, or a deity or what not — but it ain't so with a cat. A cat ain't servant nor slave to anybody at all. He's got all the independence there is, in Heaven or anywhere else, there ain't any left over for anybody else. He's your friend, if you like, but that's the limit — equal terms, too, be you king or be you cobbler; you can't play any I'm-better-than-you on a cat — no, sir! Yes, he's your friend, if you like, but you got to treat him like a gentleman, there ain't any other terms. The minute you don't, he pulls freight.
– **Mark Twain**

Sunday, January 27, 1884. — There was another story in the paper a week or so since. A gentleman had a favourite cat whom he taught to sit at the dinner table where it behaved very well. He was in the habit of putting any scraps he left onto the cat's plate. One day puss did not take his place punctually, but presently appeared with two mice, one of which it placed on its master's plate, the other on its own.
– **Beatrix Potter**, *Journal*

---

[189] What sort indeed?

Confront a child, a puppy, and a kitten with a sudden danger; the child will turn instinctively for assistance, the puppy will grovel in abject submission, the kitten will brace its tiny body for a frantic resistance.

– **Saki**

Everyone has noticed the taste which cats have for pausing and lounging between the two leaves of a half-shut door. Who is there who has not said to a cat, 'Do come in!' There are men who, when an incident stands half-open before them, have the same tendency to halt in indecision between two resolutions, at the risk of getting crushed through the abrupt closing of the adventure by fate. The over-prudent, cats as they are, and because they are cats, sometimes incur more danger than the audacious.'

– **Victor Hugo,** *Les Misérables*

One of the most poignant cat tales and perhaps my favourite is 'The Cat That Walked by Himself' by Rudyard Kipling: 'He walked by himself, and all places were alike to him... waving his wild tail and walking his wild lone.' One critic described it as Kipling's masterpiece. You can judge for yourself at https://thoughtplay. com/cat/.

I hope that you now know a little bit more about cats than when you started, and, if it is possible, love them just a tiny bit more. I would like to leave with a motto by which I live my life: Never pass a cat without stroking it.[190]

---

[190] Assuming that the cat is happy to be stroked.

About the Author

Paul Lenz is an executive at a charitable trust which focuses on evidence-led philanthropy, particularly in sub-Saharan Africa. In his spare time he can found climbing, playing fire croquet at Burning Man or befriending cats, but rarely all at once. He is the co-author of the quiz book *How Many Hippos?*. Find out about his new book – and take the quiz – at www.officehostages.com.

Printed in Great Britain
by Amazon

51227278R00090